"...*we will soon return to our tomorrow, behind us,
where we were young in love's beginning,
playing* Romeo and Juliet
and learning Shakespeare's *language...*"

—*mahmoud darwish*

The Teacher Diaries

romeo & juliet

callie feyen

ts T. S. Poetry Press • New York

T. S. Poetry Press
Ossining, New York
tspoetry.com

© 2018, Callie Feyen.

Some names in this text have been changed to preserve privacy.

Cover image by Sonia Joie
http://soniajoie.com

ISBN 978-1-943120-21-5

Library of Congress Cataloging-in-Publication Data:
Feyen, Callie
        [Nonfiction/Education/Memoir.]
        The Teacher Diaries: Romeo & Juliet/Callie Feyen
        ISBN 978-1-943120-21-5
        Library of Congress Control Number: 2018931161

To the 8th graders who were "both/and," and to the 8th graders who were my grizzly bears. I love you.

—callie feyen

Contents

Prelude to a Kiss

Do you remember what it was like? To read *Romeo & Juliet* in school for the first time? I do. Painfully so.

There was the question of who would read Juliet. There was the equally tenuous question of who would read Romeo. This kind of thing could mark the rise or fall of the teens in the room. God forbid that the teacher should pair the cute girl with the geeky boy, or vice versa.

Did that teacher have any idea about the power he held, in this seemingly simple casting choice?

I'm not sure if he did, because I was just one of the teens in the room, keeping my head down in the hopes of preserving my dignity.

Still, now, the years stretching between that first teen reading and my grown-up sensibilities, I imagine the awkwardness might not have belonged only to we-the-teens. Maybe the teacher could feel it too. If he kept a diary, I could know once and for all. His secret thoughts might be almost as intriguing as the play itself. Perhaps more so.

What *do* teachers feel when facing William Shakespeare, tales of family feud, breathless kissing scenes—all in front of a class of teens who are keeping their heads down (and threatening to fall asleep or plot their next prank in the process)?

I will never know what my 8th grade teacher felt. He left me no diary. Educator Callie Feyen, however, has done me a favor. She has written *The Teacher Diaries: Romeo & Juliet*. It begins with a kiss. Then, page by page, it reveals her generous, hopeful, and humorous heart.

The best teachers have one—a heart, that is. It helps them use their power well.

—L.L. Barkat, author of *Rumors of Water: Thoughts on Creativity & Writing*

1

Kissing a Dragon in His Fair Cave

My first kiss happened on the porch of my best friend Celena's house. It was a Saturday night in April. I was fifteen.

Before the kiss happened, I was watching Eddie Murphy's *Delirious* with Celena and her brother Andres. *Delirious* is raunchy and hilarious, and the three of us knew almost every line of Murphy's stand-up routine. We were laughing so hard I wasn't sure we'd breathe again.

The night Neal kissed me, he was no longer with Celena. But they had dated. For a while. Like, they were in love. I knew this. Most of Oak Park, Illinois knew this. And since I'm already walking into awkward territory, I may as well be completely honest and explain that I saw Andres just about every day, and he was quiet and funny and I didn't mind watching him play basketball with his friends. I don't think he minded that I was watching, either.

So the three of us are listening to Eddie Murphy tell a story about running after an ice-cream truck, and the stage lights are reflecting off his red leather pants when Neal knocks on the door looking for me, and the next thing I know I'm standing outside, my back to the little Episcopal church that's kitty-corner to Celena's house, looking into Neal's eyes and inhaling all the Drakkar he'd put on. You know what happens next.

How could I do this to Celena? She was crushed when she and Neal broke up. You know those phrases, "together through thick and thin" and "two peas in a pod"? That was Celena and me. Plus, there was something unsaid with Andres, and I go and kiss his sister's ex-boyfriend outside his house in the middle of one of the greatest stand-up comedy shows of all time. How could I let this happen?

I'll tell you how. Neal had a haircut like no other boy I knew. It was spiky and shaggy and messy and I used to stare at it in Mr. Brocks' 8th-grade English class. I'd wonder how Neal got it like that and why the other boys wouldn't do the same with their hair. (We girls were all curling our bangs so it looked like we had giant caterpillars sleeping on our foreheads. Somebody cool and beautiful obviously started that trend, and we followed suit just as fast as we could kick off our jelly shoes and buy some Aqua Net®.)

Neal was an artist. He drew on everything. His homework, his shoes, his textbooks. When he wrote me notes, he always included cartoon guys—silly and scary—in the margins. My first crush was Wil Wheaton's character in the movie *Stand By Me*. All my friends were into Cory Feldman and River Pheonix. Not me. I liked the storyteller, the quiet artist. Neal told stories with his cartoons and I liked that.

Finally, there was the Howard Jones T-shirt. That's right, Howard Jones. The one whose songs you probably hear when you're getting a cavity filled. Sometimes, Neal wore a Howard Jones concert tour shirt to school and I lost my mind. It was black with white print and a thick, light blue stripe that was off-center. I could think of nothing else the days he wore his Howard Jones T-shirt.

But I didn't pine for Neal. At least, not while he was dating Celena. He and I were in a lot of the same classes together, though, and we were buddies. When they broke up, and I found out he was interested in me, it was hard for me to resist those blue eyes, that reckless hair, and that Howard Jones T-shirt.

Still, I was a good kid, and I knew better. What I did made no sense. Also, Celena knew all this. I told her how I felt about Neal, and she was the one who told me he liked me. She opened the door that Saturday night and pushed me outside with a smile on her face. After, she celebrated my first kiss like only a best friend could.

Two years later, I was at Celena's, sitting at her dining room table, sobbing over a different boy. When he broke up with me he told me I was monotonous—a word I had to look up in the dictionary. In those days, I wrote the date next to all the words I looked up and 12/5/92 is next to *monotonous*: "tedious, boring, dull, uninteresting, unexciting." You get the picture. I learned the definition one day before my 17th birthday.

That boy immediately started dating someone else—a girl I knew, who seemed nice. Celena was in the kitchen with the refrigerator door open when I asked, "Is this how you felt when I did this to you?" She looked at me, shocked. I held her stare for a moment and then said, "I'm sorry."

I don't remember what she said. I know she didn't say, "That's okay," or, "I'm your best friend no matter what." That was never Celena's style. What I do remember is this: Celena wordlessly walking over to the table where I was and putting a tub of Cool Whip between us. She handed me a candy cane, and she opened up a bag of Chex Mix™ and sat down, and together we ruined our dinner.

I cannot justify or explain one bit of my behavior on that porch, but I can remember, very clearly, all the feelings: how hard I was laughing at Eddie Murphy, that mellow, sweet emotion of hanging out with friends that are as close as family, the way my stomach flipped when Neal knocked on the door, the heavy feeling I had standing with him in the dark, the way my eyes stung and my stomach hollowed out when I said I'm sorry to Celena.

I suppose someone could argue what I felt wasn't really love, but I did feel something. Perhaps it was a sort of love. No matter. It was colorful, and vivid, and electric, and I relished whatever it was. I think being a teenager is like tasting cinnamon gum for the first time and realizing what taste buds are. We know sour and sweet, spicy and salty, but not like this.

In the introduction to *Romeo and Juliet*, the Oxford University Press explains that when we first meet Juliet she's talking with her father about marriage. A young man named Paris is asking for Juliet's hand, and her father wants to know what she thinks. The last sentence in this paragraph reads: "She hasn't given much thought to the subject, but she's an obedient child, and she promises to give serious consideration to the man her parents have found for her."

When I teach *Romeo and Juliet*, I use this edition, and it is the next one-sentence paragraph I make sure my students and I discuss:

"And then she meets Romeo."

I think this is a sentence that's felt before it's understood. Like the events leading up to a first kiss; perhaps the kiss itself. I also think it's a sentence that ought to be studied, though it may not be as exciting as sitting cross-legged on the floor with your best friend as she asks, "Okay, what happened then? What'd he do then?" Still, I pursue it.

I tell my students that when I was in school, my teachers told me you don't start a sentence with *and*, and paragraphs are made up of three to five sentences.

"I was also told," I explain, "that if you are going to break a rule, you better know why you're doing it." Then I ask why the rules were broken for this pivotal five-word fragment.

"Something's changed," one student might say. "Something's different."

I tell the students this sentence is supposed to feel dramatic because what's happened to Juliet is dramatic. Here she is, following all the rules, happy to consider the suggestions of her parents, and then something happens. *Someone* happens.

"Has this ever happened to you?" I'll ask. Nobody will answer, but several students will smile.

"I was in 5th grade when it happened to me," I'll offer, "and I was in Sunday School." This usually gets the class laughing and riled. Of all the places to meet Romeo, it probably shouldn't be in church.

But that's the thing about love. It shows up suddenly, and there's nothing you can do to stop it. I think we waste time arguing over whether what Romeo and Juliet felt was truly love. They felt something, and it was real and that's where the story is.

My confession relaxes my classes. They're entering an awkward, confusing, romantic story with someone who's been there. If I had started the lesson stating that Romeo and Juliet were two melodramatic teenagers who made a giant mess of things, I would've sent a message that if my students ever had (or have) an "And then she meets Romeo" moment, something is wrong with them. They're wrong for feeling what they're feeling. They can't possibly understand what love is and how to handle it.

When do we ever understand what love is and how to handle it? Can you help it when love strikes? Perhaps we're better suited to study what love does, rather than how it ought to be managed.

Love breaks rules. We learn this in the introduction, but also in understanding who Romeo and Juliet are: enemies. "My only love sprung from my only hate," Juliet wails when she learns Romeo is a Montague.

Love puts us at a loss for words: "It is my lady, O it is my love:" Romeo gasps at the sight of Juliet. But then, he cannot finish the couplet: "O that she knew she were!"

And in one of my favorite passages in the entire play, Juliet shows us how love messes with our thoughts:

O serpent heart, hid with a flow'ring face!
Did ever dragon keep so fair a cave?
Beautiful tyrant, fiend angelical!
Dove-feather'd raven, wolvish-ravening lamb!
Despisèd substance of divinest show!
Just opposite to what thou justly seem'st,
A damnèd saint, an honourable villain!
O nature, what hadst thou to do in hell
When thou didst bower the spirit of a fiend
In mortal paradise of such sweet flesh?
Was ever book containing such vile matter

So fairly bound? O that deceit should dwell
In such a gorgeous palace!

Indeed, I know all about serpent hearts with flow'ring faces. I'm certain I've danced with beautiful tyrants and probably gotten into the cars of a few honourable villains. The dragon might be handsome and keep a swanky cave, but he is still a dragon. We are playing with fire. I'm interested in the stories that come from the burns.

I like to teach *Romeo and Juliet* in February because love is on the brains (and hearts) of my students (even more so than normal). I pass out candy message hearts and red construction paper and tell them they have to create at least two couplets using the words on the hearts.

"These are so cheesy!" they'll complain. "Yes, they are," I'll say.

"Some of these messages are totally inappropriate!" they'll tell me, and I agree to that. "Use what you got," I encourage them.

Use the awkward. Use the inappropriate. Use the confusion and use the brand new spring air of an April Saturday night. Use the cheap cologne and the Episcopal church and use the blue eyes that shine in the night. Use the late apology and the bag of Chex Mix shared between friends.

I think that's what Shakespeare is doing with this play. He could have made Romeo and Juliet older. In fact, they were older in the original poem by Arthur Brooke. Instead, he gives two teen kids this love story, and we begin the play with two boys comparing their private parts and what they'd like to do to women with them. (*Delirious* had nothing on Shakespeare.)

If we're going to teach *Romeo and Juliet*, it's good to know about iambic pentameter and reverse metaphor. It's good to understand the motives of Tybalt and Paris. It's important to see the deep hatred the Montagues and Capulets have for one another. But it is equally important to understand what love does, and I only know how to do that by remembering what it's done to me.

Romeo and Juliet is a tragic story. The tragedy lies in the double suicide, of course, but it also lies in the fact that the two of them don't have a chance to see if anything can grow from their frantic love.

A student I once had wrote, "Nothing beautiful has no scars," and I think about the friendship I have with Celena. The two of us met when we were Juliet's age. We have shared so many laughs and secrets and big life events, including a first kiss. Neal has her first kiss, too. "It makes the story of our lives even better!" Celena told me when I brought this tidbit up recently.

I agree, even though I still can't explain why I did what I did (other than the fact that Neal was wearing that damn Howard Jones T-shirt that night). Sometimes there's nothing to explain except to sit across the table from one another, share a bag of Chex Mix, and dip candy canes into Cool Whip. Two burned, beautiful girls—marked by Romeo.

2

Dancing With Frankenstein

My daughters Hadley and Harper have been playing the piano song "Dancing with Frankenstein." It's a tune that wasn't assigned. They found it when flipping through their lesson book one afternoon. My guess? The title intrigued them.

Harper played it first. I was in the kitchen washing dishes and I shut the water off immediately. Something about the melody caught me. There's a hesitant assurance to the first few notes—a sort of hauntedness that draws you in. The second bar is played with both hands and the harmony is strong, the beat steady, inviting us to dance.

"I love that," I told Harper, as I wiped my hands on the dishtowel hanging on the oven door. "Play it again."

The song is just a warm-up to get their fingers loose, but it shows what music can do: stun, startle, soothe, crush, excite, devastate. And, through mood, music tells a story. In the case of *Romeo and Juliet*, music goes one step further and can help a story make sense.

If you've been in a room with 8th graders, you know the energy. Good or rowdy, or a mixture of both, tensions are high, and patience is thin. Get them at the end of the day, and it's like teaching in fire. The best thing, perhaps the only thing, I know to do is to stand in the tension with them and start small. When we look at the prologue of *Romeo and Juliet*, I ask my students to find and circle as many forms of "two" as they can.

> Two households, both alike in dignity,
> In fair Verona, where we lay our scene,
> From ancient grudge break to new mutiny,
> Where civil blood makes civil hands unclean.
> From forth the fatal loins of these two foes
> A pair of star-cross'd lovers take their life;
> Whose misadventured piteous overthrows
> Do with their death bury their parents' strife.
> The fearful passage of their death-mark'd love,
> And the continuance of their parents' rage,
> Which but their children's end, nought could remove,
> Is now the two hours' traffic of our stage;
> The which if you with patient ears attend,
> What here shall miss, our toil shall strive to mend.

Students find "two households" and "both alike" in line one. There's a pair of "civils" in the fourth line, and "two foes" in the fifth. Some notice there are two words beginning with *d*: *doth*, and *death*. Others find a double set of *f*'s in line five: "From forth the fatal loins of these two foes." (Usually we have to pause and clatter on about the word *loins*. In my professional opinion, it's best to let them giggle or it only gets worse.) Some play around with opposites and find: "death mark'd love." Others notice every other line rhymes: dignity, mutiny, scene, unclean.

"So what do we know?" I'll ask.

"Two families hate each other," one student might say.

"Two kids from those families fall in love," another adds. "Both kids die."

"This play will take two hours," one student always says, then looks at the calendar I have hanging on the wall. "So, does that mean we'll be done with this play by Wednesday?" he'll ask hopefully.

They've gathered a lot from their search of two, so I move on to the components of a sonnet and how to mark iambic pentameter. Then, I turn to music.

It's been my experience that most adolescents are not eager to read aloud a story if they're unsure of it. Their trepidation could be because of content, their fear of mispronouncing words, or lack of interest. William Shakespeare can be a monster that they have no interest in dancing with. Music can be the beat that helps them forget or perhaps disregard their fear and step onto the dance floor.

My favorite part of the movie *Footloose* (the one with Kevin Bacon) is the night Ren and friends go to an out-of-town bar that allows dancing (the horror!). Sarah Jessica Parker's character is dating a boy who thinks he can't dance, and feels stupid because of it, so she promises to sit with him while Ren and his girlfriend with the red cowboy boots tear it up on the dance floor.

That is, until she can't help herself. The scene makes me cry every time. First, she's sitting on a bar edge, kicking her feet to the beat. Then, she raises her arms and sort of shifts her ribs side to side along to John Cougar Mellencamp's "Hurts So Good." Finally, she jumps off the ledge and skips to the middle of the dance floor, smiling and dancing. "I'm sorry!" she yells back at Sean Penn's brother. "I just can't help it!" I cry because I know exactly what she means. I want to capture music's pull in my classroom.

Students line up in rows of two, each holding a copy of the Prologue. I tell the class I will play music and they are to walk and read, matching the tone and the beat both in words and movement.

The first song I play is Muse's "Uprising." The song has a rumbling pulse and I imagine motorcycles at night, stomping feet, and fists clenched. Students read the Prologue's lines in a biting staccato as they march down the line.

The second song I play is "Passion Chorale" from Bach's *St. Matthew Passion*, sung by the Ambrosian Singers. I turn off the lights, light a candle, and students repeat the same exercise. The words have not changed but the students step carefully, somberly as they introduce this star-crossed love that will eventually end Romeo and Juliet's lives.

After this activity, students take out a piece of notebook paper and write a summary of what they understand of the play so far after reading the Prologue. I also tell them to share any questions they have. Their responses range from basic, "I understand the play is written in iambic pentameter," to complex, "Why couldn't Juliet talk to her parents about this? I think my parents would want to know."

I probably could've taught this without the music, but I think it's important to feel a story even if we don't understand every aspect of it.

Every day I hear "Dancing with Frankenstein," I think not of the creature in Mary Shelley's story, but of its creator, Victor Frankenstein. It is *him* the song is referring to, though I bet my girls think the song is about the being he allowed to turn into a monster. When they play, I wonder if they imagine dancing with something they are afraid of or something they doubt they should hold hands with.

Now that they know the notes, they're testing what it is they can do, and the melody is too strong to resist. Like Sarah Jessica Parker in *Footloose*. Like Romeo and Juliet. Like me, who left the dirty dishes and a dishrag haphazardly folded on the oven's door because I didn't want to miss a beat. Like Victor Frankenstein, a romantic who didn't concern himself with the consequences. He only wanted to dance.

3

Pernicious Rage

The Oak Park and River Forest High School Food Fight of 1993 happened on a Friday. I remember, because I was wearing my Drill Team uniform, and I always wore my Drill Team uniform on Fridays. There was a basketball game that night. I know this because the Varsity players had on khakis, button-downs, and ties. It was lunchtime. That part is probably obvious.

I was sitting with my Drill Team teammates. Like every day, I took out all the contents of my brown paper bag: a bagel and cream cheese sandwich, celery and carrots, an orange, my mom's cookies, and a Diet Coke®. I folded my lunch bag nice and neat and put my food on it.

The basketball team sat behind us. In front of us sat Crew. As in Stage Crew. One of the Crew boys was my next-door neighbor. He had long, black hair that was always in his face. His bedroom was in the basement of his house, and at night when I came home, blue light beamed across our backyards and heavy metal music that I thought sounded like a chainsaw trying to start pulsated from his room. He and I never said a word to each other.

So it's Crew, Drill Team, and the basketball team, and as far as I knew, we were all happily eating our lunches. I remember my friend Melissa was delicately patting the grease off a cafeteria chocolate chip cookie (we all loved them), while she and I analyzed the actions of the boys we were currently interested in. I remember another girl, Karyn, was telling us the trick to get our nails to grow was to paint them a different color every day.

I don't remember a shift in the air, or a hush in the cafeteria. I don't remember anyone yelling or swearing. What I remember is cracking open my Diet Coke—it was my favorite part of lunch, so I saved it for last. I remember lifting the can to my lips and arranging my mouth into sip formation, and even inhaling, but that day I would not partake of the artificial sweetness I so looked forward to.

In one amazing movement, the entire Crew stood up holding various foods in their hands, ready to launch. I saw the neighbor boy's face for the first time. He'd tucked his hair behind his ears and I could see how angry he was.

I didn't have time to figure out what was going on. Melissa grabbed my arm and pulled me out of my seat. "Duck and run!" she screamed, still holding my wrist and taking me with her. We ran around the perimeter of the cafeteria and out the door. "Don't look behind you!" Melissa screamed. "Just run!"

When we were safely out of the cafeteria, we turned around to have a look. Rarely have I experienced something and said, "This is exactly what it's like in the movies," but what I saw was exactly like a high school movie food fight. People were throwing sub sandwiches like footballs. I saw one kid slap orange slices like he was serving a volleyball. Another boy I knew, who was so quiet I figured he was mute, was screaming obscenities at the top of his lungs while spraying cheese from a can over his head.

"This is the basketball team's fault," Melissa said.

"Huh?" I asked. "Crew stood up first."

"Nah," she said, brushing off food debris from her Drill Team uniform. "They were provoked. Those players were throwing food at them the whole time. They were asking for it."

Melissa and I watched while security guards rushed into the cafeteria. It would be impossible for them to pinpoint who started it or how it was started. As far as I knew, Melissa and now I were the only people who knew how it started.

I've told this story to my 8th graders after we've read the first 110 lines of Romeo and Juliet. The spines of the books are barely cracked and a fight breaks out between the Capulets and Montagues. "What in the world?" Some of the students say. "How do you just start fighting like that? Why do they hate each other so much?"

I tell them I have no idea. I tell them I don't know if the Capulets and Montagues know. I tell them the best answer I can give them is that two groups believe they are superior to one another. Or there's something different about one group that is interpreted as disgusting, rude, insulting, or weird.

"We all know what that's like, don't we?" I'll say.

"Not enough to kill!" they'll reply.

No, not enough to kill, I'll agree. But I'll bring back the food fight of '93, and I'll begin comparing some of the characters in Romeo and Juliet with the people in my story.

Melissa and I weren't as vilely suggestive as Sampson and Gregory, but we were talking about boys, and we were considering how to get their attention. And I might not have been as nasty about the neighbor boy, but my description of him made it clear I thought he was weird—scary, even.

When Abram enters the scene we can hear Sampson and Gregory plotting; they're looking for a fight, just like the basketball boys, and we all agree the Prince is like the security guards who break up the fight and tell everyone to cut it out.

I suppose, since we're female, my students associate Melissa and me with Ladies Montague and Capulet, but I tell them I think Melissa is Benvolio in this scene. She's the one who knew all the details, who saw the truth, and what's more, told it. Benvolio even tries to stop the fight and urges Tybalt to use his sword not to kill but "to part these men with me."

"What, drawn and talk of peace?" Tybalt says. "I hate the word,/As I hate hell, all Montagues, and thee."

"So is Tybalt the bad guy?" my students will ask, and in turn, they assign Benvolio the role of good guy.

"Do you think the neighbor boy was the bad guy?" I ask.

"No!" they'll say. "He was provoked!"

Soon, we aren't talking about good versus bad. We're talking about the characters and why they think the way they do. What happened to them that makes them hate so utterly and completely?

Once the students begin to see the characters as more than "good" and "bad," I pass out a *Verona Times* newspaper assignment. Here, they have a chance to review the first part of Act 1, and also get into the characters' mindsets.

Each student gets a sealed envelope with a special assignment in it: some are reporters, some are writing op-eds, some have to write exclusive interviews between Lady Montague and Lady Capulet, some create advertisements showcasing products the characters in Verona might be interested in.

I give them time to draft, and then I have the students get together in groups to produce a newspaper. With access to computers, they can use ready-made templates, but I find they bring out more inner creativity with butcher paper, markers, and glue sticks.

The idea is to try to organize and articulate a confusing, heated situation. I think if we can come at it as play, the tension of working with a story we don't completely understand minimizes.

And I think when we're playing, we have an opportunity to see more of the story. Like with the neighbor boy. Yes, his music was frightening, but after the food fight, I'd stand in my backyard a few minutes before curfew and listen—trying to catch the beat, trying to understand the melody, and realizing neither could quench the fire of the neighbor boy's pernicious rage.

4

Walking in the Sycamore Grove

I pick my older daughter Hadley up from school, and before she can get her seatbelt clicked, she tells me about a friend who won't be partners with her in gym. I do my best to stay calm and not project how I feel about this predicament onto Hadley. I try to validate her feelings, and though Hadley doesn't say anything, I can tell whatever it is I've said is not enough. She looks out the window as we pull away. She's mulling something over.

Within minutes, she picks a fight with Harper. It's what Hadley does when she's feeling lousy. I tell her to cut it out, but she doesn't, and Harper gets riled up. I get riled up, too, and soon the three of us are all storming into the house, slamming our bags on the floor, and stomping all over the place. *This was not how I wanted to handle things*, I think, as I toss empty Tupperware® into the kitchen sink.

I look out the window above the faucet and study the trees in and by our backyard. We have three. They have sturdy trunks, perfect for sitting against on a warm afternoon. We haven't lived in this house for long, but already the girls have claimed one as their own. It's a climbing tree, and a shade tree, and it's a tree they collect treasure underneath. I wonder if this will be the tree they grow up with precisely because it stands just outside our property. They know where home is, but they need a place to gather memories, thoughts, and feelings, like the sticks and pine cones that are lying in bunches at the roots. They need a place to turn these treasures over.

There is a tree in *Romeo and Juliet*, too. After the brawl in Scene 1, after Prince Escalus reprimands the Capulets and Montagues and tells him he'll kill the next person who starts a fight, everyone takes a deep breath and Lady Montague wonders where her son Romeo is.

Benvolio, Romeo's buddy, tells her that both he and Romeo have been walking around in the dark with troubled minds. Benvolio walked to the west side of the city where the sycamore trees grow, and it was there he spotted Romeo, though Romeo wanted to be alone.

"I," Benvolio explains to Romeo's mother, "measuring his affections by my own,/which then most sought where most might not be found,/Being one too many by my weary self,/Pursu'd my humour, not pursuing his,/And gladly shunn'd who gladly fled from me."

The two boys just wanted solitude in the sycamore grove.

In class, I have my students think about the kind of tree Shakespeare placed in this scene.

"What does *amore* mean?" I ask.

"Love," they respond.

"What does *syc* sound like?"

"Sick."

It's easy to assume at first glance that such white-barked trees with shredded trunks are dying, but they are very much alive. I believe anyone between the age of 10 and 15 knows what it means to be misunderstood, as well as the trouble it takes to understand. Being very much alive is no easy business. I don't pass up the significance of the sycamore tree in my classes, or its placement on the edge of town—a place to wander when you are a little lost.

I also discuss Shakespeare's use of contrasts. Love and sick seem incompatible, but together they make a word we can feel: blushing cheeks, fidgety limbs, sweaty palms, catching breath. We know these symptoms well.

Later, when Benvolio and Romeo meet up, we see what Shakespeare can really do with dichotomies, making *lovesick* look like child's play.

"O heavy lightness, serious vanity,/Misshapen chaos of well-seeming forms,/Feather of lead, bright smoke, cold fire,/ sick health/still-waking sleep …"

I have students illustrate one of these pairs, as well as come up with a set themselves: hopeful mystery, perfect confusion, and blurry focus are some of what they offer.

I want my students to see that love does something. That is, love *acts* in *Romeo and Juliet*. It has a large role in this play. Working with contrasts, as Shakespeare did, helps students get at this wonderful bafflement, this terrifyingly-sweet enigma.

I ask students to think of love as a character, and one activity that helps tease this idea out is writing a "Bio Poem," a poem that summarizes who a person is. The directions are simple. Each line answers a question: What is the person's first name? What did this person accomplish? What feelings did this person have? For example, one student wrote:

Love.
Explosive, magical, can't be
Rushed.

Mother, Father, Family,
Friend.
Lover of my soul.
It feels scary and strange.
Love fears not being
returned.
Love brings marriage and families.
Love wants to see
You succeed.
Lives inside those
Who have fallen in it.
Never Ending.

Here, I am trying to show students that love is a character in this play. A sweltering, menacing, playful, delightful, taunting character.

Their work is sincere. They are close to these symptoms that love spreads. Some students have experienced them already, and like Romeo, it is hard to feel anything else than the heavy lightness of lovesickness. We are deep in the grove of sycamores.

I wonder about this time spent with the sycamores as I watch my daughters by the tree just beyond our yard, during this season when the winter weather is teasing in spring. Right now, Hadley's learning the impossible rules of friendships with girls—perhaps more difficult than what she'll experience when she falls in love for the first time.

I wish there was something I could do, and I realize that I'm afraid of the sycamore's siren call. In *Romeo and Juliet*, Romeo's father, Montague, tells Benvolio my same message:

"Could we but learn from whence his sorrows grow,/we would as willingly give cure as know." I think, though, that Mr. Montague has it wrong. There isn't much either of us can do. Heartbreak and heartache always feel fresh, no matter how many times they happen. I'm not sure I could give a cure even if Hadley asked me to.

Hadley reaches for a branch that's just past her fingertips, her T-shirt raising, exposing her belly. She jumps and grasps the branch, swinging. I see her smiling. Harper jumps in exuberance at Hadley's accomplishment, and then begins to try. She can't reach no matter how high she jumps, so Hadley drops to the ground, and picks Harper up so she can feel what it's like to swing from the branch of their beloved tree. I think of Benvolio walking alongside Romeo, asking him what is wrong. Romeo says it's all too sad to tell Benvolio what the matter is. "Tell me in sadness," Benvolio encourages Romeo.

Harper won't let go of the branch once she's on it. She hangs and hangs and hangs while Hadley jumps up and holds on, jumps up and holds on.

I take down three plates from the cupboard, and pull a box of graham crackers from the pantry. I slather Nutella® on the crackers, and toss rainbow sprinkles on the chocolate. I pour glasses of milk and call the girls in and to our kitchen table. The three of us quietly munch our snack.

I take a deep breath. My girls smell of outside: of sweat and leaves and dirt and of spring that's on its way. I love that they smell of growth and of what's coming. And I feel a sting of joy-sorrow for my very much alive young ladies.

5

"Where's My Daughter? Call Her Forth"

It's a few nights before Christmas. My mom and I are in the kitchen in the house I grew up in on Gunderson, near Chicago. She's moving about, pulling food from the fridge, lifting plates out of cupboards, setting out napkins and wine glasses.

I'm standing in the same place I've always stood since my parents re-did the kitchen when I was 14, at the counter that opens to the dining room. I can see the outside—the oak trees, the streetlights that flickered on well before the 6 o'clock rush of Oak Park residents walking home from the El. December in the Midwest grows dark early. You can feel it at 3:30; the heavy cold presses on your shoulders as the barely blue sky fades quickly to grey, and then a crystal black so cold it's like walking into ice. The streetlights shine for those returning from the city, and the night glimmers.

I am a brand-new mama. My daughter, Hadley, is two months old and asleep upstairs. My mom is basking in first-time grandma-ness like a gal who's just been asked for her hand in marriage. She is effervescent, and soon Hadley will be up and friends will be over, the wine will be poured, and the house will be pulsing with celebratory oohs and aahs as Hadley is passed around.

My mom puts hummus and olives, cheese and crackers on a wooden slab in front of me. The library lights next door turn off for the evening, except for the security lights that cast a glow on the books like a blanket. I can see those lights and the books through my bedroom window. The Els rush by quickly now and I think they're cold, too. I wonder about checking on Hadley when the door opens. It is Mrs. Carlson.

"Are you ready to laugh your ass off?" she asks, removing her gloves ever so daintily.

"Always," my mom says, uncorking the wine and pouring a glass for her dear friend.

My mom and Mrs. Carlson have been friends since her daughter, Sarah, and I met our freshman year of high school. While Sarah and I had done our fair share of teenage girl mischief, my mom and Mrs. Carlson were known to get rowdy as well. And they did it in public.

The two of them used to rollerblade around town, with this ridiculous equipment on. They were known to blade all the way to the high school football field, where Sarah and I were frequently practicing our Drill Team routines. They'd yell hello as loud as they could. Neither of them knew how to stop so they'd roll and usually fall onto the grass, or crash into a fence, resulting in howls of laughter.

"Our moms are here," I'd tell Sarah between clenched teeth, not moving a muscle in their direction.

"Oh my gosh," Sarah would say, following suit. "Ignore them."

You couldn't ignore either of them, though. Nobody could. They were a force: a loud, incredibly witty, stunningly stylish force.

"Callie, sweetie," Mrs. Carslon says as she makes her way towards where I'm standing. I smile and watch her expectantly.

She puts her hands on either side of my face, and the smile she's giving me seems to lift her hair. "You're a mama!" The way she says it makes me feel like I've done something, like I *am* something.

She lifts her glass. "Cheers," she says, and my mom and I reciprocate, then Mrs. Carlson goes on to tell us a story that, indeed, has us laughing so hard, we could count it as cardio.

It's easy to wince when reading the Nurse's debut scene. In fewer than fifty lines, we learn of her daughter's death, and she shares the very palpable details of how she weaned Juliet, as well as her body's reaction to that weaning. We learn that her husband is also gone, and we hear a little anecdote about Juliet's toddler years. After my first reading of the Nurse's speech, I wrote in the margin, "Girlfriend could've started a blog."

Shakespeare's Nurse is off-color, and she gives far more information than she needs to. She is also the person Juliet trusts most. When I teach *Romeo and Juliet* and we get to this part in the play, before we read, I give my students a warning.

"She says way too much, and she might make you squirm a bit."

This, of course, makes them want to read on. Dangle any hint of something taboo in front of a middle school student, and they'll devour it.

I go on to explain, though, that I believe it is her stories, perhaps even the inappropriate and overloaded details of her stories, that make Juliet trust her and tell her things.

"She's kind of like me," I tell my students, and they look at me, shocked at the comparison.

"C'mon," I'll say, "you know I have a story for everything."

They laugh, thinking they are the ones who throw me off course, taking up class time, when I meticulously plan for it. I offer my stories—my vulnerable, awkward, growing-up stories—because I'm leveling the playing the field. I want to bear some of what it is my students are going through so they will trust themselves to get at their stories. I'm attempting to pull something out of them, as the Nurse does for Juliet, as Mrs. Carlson has done for me.

The opening line in Act 1, Scene 3 is a question and a command. "Where's my daughter?" Lady Capulet asks the Nurse. "Call her forth to me." We can interpret that line literally. Mrs. Capulet doesn't know where her kid is and is asking the Nurse to help find her.

I think this line can be interpreted figuratively as well. That is, we mothers don't always understand what's going on with our children—their experience is not our own. Recognizing this can be scary, when we see them on the brink of adolescence, marriage, motherhood. Where's the daughter we once knew? Who is she now? How much of this experience do we help her navigate? How do we help her become who she's going to be? Why not bring in our friends to call forth something in our children.

Before Lady Capulet tells Juliet to "Read o'er the volume of young Paris' face,/And find delight writ there with beauty's pen," before Juliet falls for Romeo on the night she is to look at Paris, before the Nurse and the Friar take part in this star-crossed romance, let's look at the Nurse in all her vibrant, story-telling glory. Let's watch her and Juliet together, then nod along with Lady Capulet when she tells the Nurse to "come back again,/ I have remember'd me," because it can be our friends who not only call forth something in our children, but help us remember a part of ourselves we've forgotten.

Mrs. Carlson, my mom, and I stand together in the kitchen for a few minutes before the rest of the company arrives— these two women sharing the space where I'd been listening to and wondering about the night, each of them with an arm on my shoulders, making me laugh.

Hadley wakes up, and I bring her downstairs to show her to friends who've watched me grow up. There's Mrs. Padour, who made pancakes in the shape of my initials while her daughters and I watched, sleepy-eyed from staying up too late, and happy from the sizzle of buttermilk and flour, eggs and vanilla shaping itself into a perfectly fluffy *C*. There's Mrs. Roldan, who, on a Saturday night when Celena and I were broken-hearted over a boy, sat with us on her bed and told us her own broken-hearted boy stories. Mrs. Todd is here, too. She gave me one of my first jobs, helping her sell tea in her tea store. I loved lifting the big glass jars, gently scooping up jasmine, Ceylon, or, my favorite, cinnamon spice tea leaves and spilling them into golden bags for customers. And at lunch time, Mrs. Todd and I would sip Diet Coke® and eat our sandwiches and giggle about one thing or another we found silly. Now Mrs. Carlson is smiling, her eyes twinkling, and I think she's coming up with her next story. Mom smiles, too.

All of them, like the Nurse, calling me forth.

6

Wild Mercutio

Before they met Mercutio, I taught my 8th graders how to play Pac-Man. It's basically tag on a basketball court, but you can only run along the lines. Whoever gets chomped by Pac-Man is out.

I wasn't planning this with my class, but a few things happened that week, and by the time Friday rolled around, I decided we all needed to participate in a little folly before we hung out with the ultimate fool, albeit a fool I knew would steal our hearts and then break them.

The first thing that happened was that I yelled at my students. In my defense, this particular group of 8th graders was notorious for its obnoxious, belligerent ways. Everything was a joke. Everything was innuendo. I was actually looking forward to introducing them to Mercutio because I figured they'd think they'd found a friend, and while I wasn't too confident they'd learn to be respectful, maybe Mercutio could teach them how to speak with wit, and not go for the obvious joke. After all, part of the fun in a snide remark is creating how it'll be delivered.

But they'd gotten on my last nerve with their paper throwing, their talking when I was talking, their sauntering into class whenever they felt like it, always with an excuse. I'd had it, and I let them know it.

What really got to me, I told them while I paced the room like a lioness ready to pounce, was how thoughtful and creative they all were. "But you're all so scared," I yelled. "You're afraid to try so you cover up what *could be* with this bullshit."

I dismissed class early, and drove home angry and crying.

Second, that evening, I received an email from a parent. I braced myself for getting reprimanded for swearing in class as I clicked open the message. This woman's son was one of those All-American boys—great at sports, tall, blond, and an artist. Except he didn't want anyone to know the artist part. It seeped from him, though. It was in his handwriting, in the margins of his reading homework, in the sentences he didn't mean to write but couldn't help. His work revealed so much. His mother knew this, too.

"Sometimes they don't know," she to wrote me. They don't realize how confused and afraid they are, or they do, and they don't know what to do about it. She told me, gently, that I have to show them. Over and again, I have to show them. It's exhausting.

I let out a sigh as I finished the email, and considered Mercutio. Who had given up on him? Who had dismissed him before he was ready to be let go? What of his character was he afraid to reveal, but it seeped from his words anyway?

It was spring. It was here, or it was coming; nobody can ever be sure in March, but the world was getting ready for it. The branches were nubby and green with raw growth; the trees' bark was warm in the afternoons. The mud was sloppy and gushy and we dragged in more grass and dirt than we did snow. The air still had a nip to it, but it smelled like it was turning over, like something else was on its way. So much around me seemed to be saying, "Hush, hush. Wait. Look carefully. Things you cannot see are happening."

The swearing, the email, and the mysterious beginnings of spring were what led me to take my 8th graders to a park with a basketball court and teach them how to play Pac-Man. We'd play, and then we'd meet Mercutio.

On the whiteboard that afternoon were three short sentences by Mary Oliver: *Pay Attention. Be Astonished. Tell About it.*

"We're going on a walk, and I'm going to teach you how to play Pac-Man," I told them. They shifted in their seats and giggled in anticipation.

"Take out a piece of notebook paper and a pen or pencil, and copy these sentences down at the top of your paper. When we get back, you will fill up this page, front and back, with what happened."

With that, we left the school and took a short walk to a park across the street.

The air was crisp, and we needed jackets, but the sun was out and I knew that soon we'd all tie those jackets around our waists. I didn't point that out, nor did I point out the brook we crossed, making its first spring gurgles as it rushed towards who knows where. Maybe the Potomac, or the Chesapeake Bay, or the Atlantic Ocean. Who knows where these twisting tributaries push themselves.

I didn't point out how the class split up as we walked; most of the girls clumped and huddled together while the boys ran and jumped and shouted. I said very little except to give the directions to the game. I wanted my students to find astonishment for themselves, and then name it.

I watched though, and I listened, and I thought about

these students I'd known since August. *It doesn't take long to get attached to a group*, I thought, as I watched them run around the court. I was attached to this one. My concern and fondness for the classes I teach changes the way I teach. In fact, I don't think I've ever taught a story the same way more than once.

Last year's 8th graders were more like Benvolio. They were truth tellers, and concerned about one another. I chuckled as I watched this year's 8th graders shove and pull at each other. *They are my wild things. They are my Mercutios. You can't teach Mercutio the same way you teach Benvolio. Every day with these kids is a wild rumpus, and instead of trying to stop it, I need to get front and center and command its commencement.*

I was terrified to teach this group. Their reputation for being mean and rowdy proceeded them. I saw it in the hallways and heard about it from other teachers. The group I'd had the prior year was so good and I was so afraid of the one coming, I considered asking if I could follow the kids I had and teach 9th grade English, never needing to deal with this group and my fear.

I would've missed out on so much, though. One of those things would've been seeing Mercutio for more than a narcissistic rabble-rouser. Last year, my students giggled at and tsk-tsked his antics. We were sad when he died, sure, but it was more of a "he had it coming" sort of sadness.

This group pushed me to see Mercutio differently. Maybe Mercutio was ridiculous and crass because he didn't know how else to act. Or he was too afraid to act otherwise. Nobody showed him; they just called bullshit on everything he did and brushed him off as obnoxious, crude, beyond help.

It seems that part of Shakespeare's storytelling revolves

around or begins with play, and Mercutio, though he seems reckless, is the most playful character in *Romeo and Juliet*. I wanted this group of students to laugh at Mercutio, maybe even be delighted and charmed by him. I think this helps us keep looking at him, to see what else is there.

My kids were quiet once they came back into the room after Pac-Man. They settled down quickly and began to write, the smell of spring and of growing bodies lingering thickly among us. One boy wrote about the mechanics of the game and the wind on his face as he ran. Another described these bristly brown nuts that fell from the trees. He wrote that they were perfect for throwing at girls.

One of the girls wove *Hamilton* quotes throughout her entry while at the same time exploring the different friendships in the class and how they'd evolved since kindergarten. Another girl, an exchange student who didn't know a word of English at the beginning of the year, practiced capturing the dialogue of her American classmates while taking note of the cherry blossoms floating around—Japan's gift to D.C., a symbol of growing friendship and a sure sign spring is here.

Some boys wrote about being the fastest runners to get to the court, and then acknowledged that there was nothing to do but wait once the glory of winning a race nobody declared but them was over. Other boys wrote about wishing they could keep up, and this led them to heftier topics: keeping up with homework, being popular, being cool. Many wrote about wanting to jump in the brook we crossed but deciding Mrs. Feyen would make the whole class go inside if they did. To this day, I'm not sure what I would've done. Sometimes I wonder if I'd have jumped in with them.

It was some of the best writing I'd seen from that class, and, as in most days of my teaching career, I was the one learning the lesson. On that day, the lesson was: step aside and let Mercutio play.

The next day, we met Mercutio. We listened as Romeo whined about being through with love while Mercutio eagerly threw on his mask to crash the Capulets' party. "If love be rough with you, be rough with love," Mercutio says. Boys guffawed, and some admitted wanting to high-five Mercutio for his philosophy. Girls gasped, and put their hands over their mouths in horror.

"Here's a guy who has a line for everything," I explained to hearty smiles and knowing glances. "We don't have anyone in this class like that," I joked.

Romeo isn't persuaded by Mercutio's boisterous energy, and isn't interested in going to the party. Instead, he wants to talk about a dream he had.

I imagine the boys standing outside the Capulets' home— music booming, smells of delicious food wafting through the air, beautiful people walking past, ready to party. I imagine Mercutio observing this too, and rolling his eyes at Romeo's behavior. "Seriously, Romeo," Mercutio might say today, "you want to talk about a dream when we're about to crash a party?"

This is one of my favorite scenes in the play because I think it captures the quick wit of teenage boys and how much fun they are to be around. It was in high school that my brother and I got along the best. Part of that had to do with the fact that I stopped bossing him around, but I also remember Geoff and his friends' roughhousing, nonstop wrestling, crashing into everything, let's-see-who-can-burp-the-loudest behavior turning into a side-splitting, effortless humor that was endearing and made me forget for a while my teenage-induced drama. Geoff could take something I said in all seriousness and turn it into comedy in a blink of an eye.

Plus, Geoff and his buddies were always on the move. I can remember Saturdays: Celena and I'd be primping in my bedroom, deciding what to do that night, while Geoff and his friends had already been to the city and back and were getting ready for the next thing. Once, while Celena and I were in the kitchen eating popcorn, Geoff busted through the front door and sprinted down the basement stairs in a hysteric frenzy. Seconds later, he'd come back up with a baritone, out of breath from carrying the mother of all brass instruments up the stairs.

"What are you doing with that?" I asked in my perfect 17-year-old snotty voice.

"I'm gonna play the theme song from *Jaws* while Tim drives behind people walking down the street." Geoff started to laugh, then said, "You know how the melody gets faster? Well, Tim will speed up the car while I play, 'Duh, duh. Duh, duh. Duh, duh,' faster and faster!" He put the baritone down because he was laughing so hard.

"Oh. My. God," Celena said.

"That is so dumb," I said.

Geoff, still laughing said, "Yeah. Wanna join us?"

"Yes," Celena and I said, getting up from the table.

And so it goes with Mercutio and Romeo. When Romeo says morosely, "I dreamt a dream tonight," he's hoping Mercutio will take the bait and sit a spell with his friend to find out what this dream is all about. Mercutio plays right back: "And so did I," he says, and it is Romeo who now takes the bait. He thinks Mercutio will join him in his reverie. "Well, what was yours?" he asks.

"That dreamers often lie."

The volley between the two boys doesn't end, and Romeo bounces back another line about those who dream, sometimes "dream things true," and that is the serve that allows Mercutio's Queen Mab to take flight. Without skipping a beat, without contemplating for a second Romeo's mysterious statement about our ability to "dream things true," Mercutio launches into a forty-three-line description about his made-up fairy who affects the dreams of sleepers everywhere.

While they might not speak with the same rich language as Shakespeare's Mercutio, male students are notorious for weaving some fantastical tales explaining why their homework is not with them. So proud they are of what they've told me, so wrapped up in their stories, they always end with this: "So, can I still play in the [insert sport] game Friday night?"

And like my students who go on and on telling me about this adventurous night that prevented them from doing homework, Mercutio's Queen Mab speech does nothing to advance the plot; rather, it reveals Mercutio's character. He has a wonderful imagination, and a witty sense of humor.

Following the suggestion of *Shakespeare Set Free*, I divided the speech into sections and assigned students two to three lines to illustrate; then, we put the drawings together to discuss. I have found that drawing Shakespeare helps to understand him more, or, at the least, sit with the words a little longer.

We decided that Mercutio's Queen Mab is a fairy who

both helps and haunts. Much like Mercutio, much like my wild middle schoolers, much like me. None of us are one thing. We often feel and think and even do a multitude of things at once. Especially adolescents. They notice bristly, craggy nuts fallen from trees, pick them up, feel them tickle their palm, and simultaneously consider darting them at girls. They whisper with their friends while they wonder what happened between the girls ahead of them. Last year everything was great; they are proud, perhaps even arrogant at how strong and fast they are. And they are terrified of going to high school where they'll be weaker and slower.

This is where I wanted my students to stand—somewhere between Romeo, who believes in dreaming things true, and Mercutio, who creates a dream so magnificent and terrifying, then *poof!*, Queen Mab and her walnut of a chariot are no longer. He shrugs those forty-three wild lines as nothing more than a creation from an empty mind. Mercutio refuses to see the truth in what he's told his friend. Or maybe he doesn't have the courage to see the truth. Maybe he just wants Romeo to stop moping around and come party with him. Maybe it's all of the above.

At least, that's how it is in my classroom.

I think that, when it comes to middle school students, every day is a chance to play around with, step into, create something they're unsure about. This is risky business, figuring oneself out, and, frankly, it's safer to go in for the stupid joke, to be disruptive, to tease. For years this group had been identified as tough, and rightfully so, but that spring and with Mercutio flirting around the pages of our notebooks, I wanted them to lean towards something they might not quite believe about themselves, but hoped for. And, instead of brushing it aside after they'd thought it up, I wanted them to dream it true.

So I gave them a DIY Queen Mab assignment. They were to create a character who both helps and haunts, and write a fourteen-line sonnet in iambic pentameter, Mercutio-style. Along with their poems, they were to make a puppet for their character.

Their audience was the kindergarten class downstairs. For several days, my students worked on sonnets. They made puppets to go with their poetry, and they wrote a lesson plan to share with kindergarteners to help them understand rhyme and iambic pentameter.

Then, my students—who trip, sneer, rip stuff off walls, push, roll their eyes, check their phones when my back is turned—carried their puppets and their poems, and sat down with five-year-olds for an afternoon. They clapped out iambic pentameter together. They gave them words to practice rhyming. They asked them if they were ever afraid to do some-thing, but at the same time wanted to try it.

"What if you could make up someone who helped you do what you're afraid of?"

"Like a monster?"

"Like a fairy monster," one of my 8th graders suggested.

Kindergarteners smiled in awe of these big kids who, nor-mally, they fear for their loud and crashing ways. My 8th graders were still Mercutios, but they were softened Mercu-tios, vulnerable and gentle.

The evening before my class shared their poetry, I received another email. This time, it was the All-American Artist who wanted to talk to me. "I have a lot of missing work," he wrote.

He was right. The first three quarters he'd turned in gorgeous assignments, but this last one his name in my gradebook had zero after zero next to it. He told me he wanted to do the work, but at this point, he was so far behind he didn't think doing the work was worth it. "Maybe I'm not a poet," he said.

"Talk to me after class," I wrote back.

After my classroom emptied that day, I opened up my gradebook, and this boy and I sat down to have a look.

"You showed me you're a poet in August," I told him. "It doesn't go away because of this," I pointed to my gradebook. "Your gift is there for you to take and turn over and develop. What you decide to do with it is up to you, but your gift will never go away."

Together, we looked at what was missing.

"It's so much work," he almost whispered.

"Let's not worry about all of them," I said. "Which ones make you excited? Which ones interest you?"

He pointed to five or six, and I wrote them down. I asked him if he had everything he needed to complete these assignments. He told me he did.

I told him to show me what he could do with those assignments, and we'd go from there.

I didn't want him to give up when it got hard or confusing or scary. I couldn't promise him success, or assure him he could be a poet (though I think it's possible). However, I could show him that he'd thought up a reckless dream, and he could dream what he imagines true.

7

Tragic Give & Take

Part of my trepidation for teaching *Romeo and Juliet* had to do with the language. It takes me a good hour, a thesaurus, a dictionary, several commentaries, and a strong cup of coffee to plumb one of Shakespeare's sonnets. I didn't think I had the mental stamina to get through an entire play.

The other part of my trepidation had to do with the content: teenage misbehavior, teenage suicide. "We all know how this ends, right, guys?" I said on the first day of teaching the play. "I'm not pulling a Santa Claus moment here, am I?"

To take care of my first fear, I made sure I set aside adequate time to delve into the language—for both me and my students. That left me with the decision of how to teach this story, and it seemed there were three options: a.) Present Romeo and Juliet as a warning of what happens when we disobey our parents, or when we let hate fester inside us; b.) Teach the story like I would an algebraic equation. That is, simply show the steps to getting the problem without stopping to delve into the relationship between the numbers or how they give and take from each other in order to solve for *x*. Don't stop to wonder; or c.) Indulge in the story. Use the language to relate to students' lives and what they're going through. Immerse ourselves in the play so much that we can hear the fighting, engage in some give and take, feel Romeo and Juliet's first kiss, hold the bottle of poison.

I decided to go with option *c*. To teach *Romeo and Juliet* as a moralistic story with a warning, to teach it without emotion and wonder is to allow fear to take over my lesson plans. I didn't want any of my students to end up like Romeo and Juliet, or Tybalt, or Mercutio, or even Paris, but I also knew they have felt and acted similarly to these characters. We all have. We all know the blissful suffocation of a first crush. We have, or maybe are, a protective cousin who mistakes prejudice for honor. Mercutios abound, and for every one of them, there's a Paris—not really a bad guy, not really a good guy, not really given the chance to be either.

And while I remember my teenage years vividly and believe I carry that young Callie with me today, I also empathize with the adults in this story. It's not easy for me to pass off the Capulets, the Friar, and the Nurse as entirely self-involved, clueless and bullheaded. I see myself in them, too. I want my daughters to be happy and many times I equate *happy* with *safe*. Sometimes I don't trust myself with my own feelings when my daughters are confused or sad or crushed. When my students come to me with the drama of middle school, I want to help, but I fret about making a mess of things as the Nurse and the Friar did.

This is all to say that I believe there's good in each of these characters despite their mistakes and misjudgments, and so it is with us. Even though we are sometimes headed for tragedy, I want my students to see the good along the way. I want them to laugh with this group of characters, to roll their eyes, to shout at or defend them. I want them to participate.

Part of what makes this play a tragedy is because Shakespeare has created characters we admire and love, and he's put them in situations we relate to.

So I went with option *c*, and I decided to throw my students a masquerade party. When they walked into my classroom, they got to choose a mask to decorate. I wanted them to wear masks because I wanted to re-create the party the Capulets hosted, but I also think there is significance in the mask itself. Putting it on somehow allows space for us to forget our insecurities and definitions of who we think we are, or who we've been told we should be. I think covering up even a slight part of ourselves gives us a chance to lose our inhibitions and, in turn, we have an opportunity to ask, "What if?"

What if I wasn't shy?

What if I wasn't known as the smart kid?

What if I wasn't a Capulet?

What if I wasn't a Montague?

What would I think is beautiful?

What would I move toward?

How would I act?

Minutes before Romeo and Juliet meet, Romeo is downtrodden over Rosaline, and Juliet is dutifully looking for Paris. Romeo is not supposed to be at this party, and Juliet knows to stay away from Montagues, but once they see each other, Rosaline and Paris are forgotten, and now it is no longer a matter of who they are, but rather who they can become if they just stepped a little closer to what they think is beautiful.

I'm not saying I want my students to go against their families' wishes for who they are and how they act. What I want, though, is to give my students a chance to lose themselves in the story, then take that mask off, and see who's there.

"We're going to have a dance," I told them, and some smiled, some turned red, some said, "No, we aren't."

"Nobody is dancing with each other," I said, palms out as though I was trying to slow a Mack truck down. "We are all dancing together. I'm going to teach you a routine."

My crowning accomplishment other than my two daughters is that I was the Captain of my high school dance team. There's very little that makes me happier than a finely tuned, sharply executed, three-minute dance routine performed to a synchronized, booming beat. It doesn't take long for a class to learn this about me; plus, I look for an opportunity to dance with my students all year. The masquerade Juliet's father throws seemed like a perfect opportunity.

The routine I taught was simple. We all got in a circle, and I walked them through four eight-count measures of choreography. With our masks on, we be-bopped, we threw our hands in the air, we pivoted, we clapped, we sang along together and we laughed at the silliness of Mrs. Feyen's English class.

Even though this is an opportunity for a little rowdy mischief, I wanted my class to see that wearing a mask is a tool to make believe.

But we are in charge of what we choose to see. It is our choice whether we see differently. Not everyone can suspend his or her belief once the mask goes on. Tybalt couldn't.

He attends the party, and though he wears a mask, its magic is lost on him. He hears Romeo, a Montague, speaking, and no matter the good music, the laughter, the good food, and the pretty girls, Tybalt can't see, hear, or smell any of that through his thick coat of prejudice and hatred. "This, by his voice, should be a Montague. Fetch me my rapier, boy."

Tybalt hears a Montague, and instantly he is ready to kill.

Tybalt tells Capulet that there's a Montague at the party he's hosting, and Capulet says he is aware of this. "Young Romeo is it?" Not only does Capulet know who it is, he goes on to tell Tybalt that actually, Romeo's an upstanding citizen. "Verona brags of him/To be a virtuous and well-governed youth."

Capulet is not in a mask. He and his cousin spoke nostalgically at the beginning of this scene about their mask-wearing days, but now that they're grown men, they've put aside this flirtatious act. However, if the mask allows the party goers a chance to be someone they're not, if it allows them to see the world a little differently, Capulet's lines here show he doesn't need a mask to do that anymore.

If this long-lasting hatred between the Montagues and Capulets has been carried on by the adults over the years, here is one adult who shows signs that this feud is ridiculous—that hating an entire group of people because of their name or identity is wrong. "Take no note of him," Capulet tells Tybalt. "It is my will." In other words, leave Romeo alone; he is my guest.

It is Tybalt, a child, who chooses to carry this feud forth. "I will withdraw," I imagine him mumbling to himself, while Capulet is off crushing grapes with his friends. "[B]ut this intrusion shall,/Now seemingly sweet, convert to bitt'rest gall."

He is right. Tybalt *will* kill and he will *be* killed because of this hatred he chooses to hold on to.

So we put on our masks, and I led my students in a dance that was silly and boisterous, and got at the merriment of Act 1, Scene 5.

That was only a part of it, though. Signs of the tragedy to come ripple through this scene like the beginning of a tsunami. Though they are barely felt, and seem to make no difference, they cannot be stopped.

We were all dancing, my students and I—a give-and-take towards tragedy.

8

Hooked

They stroll into class while I'm writing Juliet's famous question, "O Romeo, Romeo, wherefore art thou Romeo?" on the whiteboard.

"O Romeo, Romeo," a couple of boys exaggerate in a high-pitched tone. "Where are you, Romeo?"

I turn around, a hand on my hip. "Juliet's not asking where Romeo is," I say. "She's wondering why the boy she's fallen for has to be a Montague." The class, still giggling from the boys' goofing around, stares at me and tries to stop smiling. I continue. "Juliet's saying it doesn't matter because *Montague* is just a name. It makes no difference as to who Romeo is."

I turn back to the board when one of the boys who pretended to be Juliet belts out the refrain from Justin Bieber's "Sorry," in which Justin asks if it's too late for him to apologize for whatever it is he's done. The class busts out in laughter. I roll my eyes.

All year, Bieber's question has been sung to me whether I'm reprimanding the kids or, as in this case, simply correcting them. It's a joke that gets funnier (to them) the more times they sing it.

I know the boy, and most likely the entire class is making fun of Bieber and his music (I think the people who like him most are women my age and maybe seven-year-old girls).

I also know that there's something about pop music that pulls kids in and has them repeating the ditties—first, because they're catchy, and second, because these words help them make sense of their lives. Justin Bieber, Ludacris, Meghan Trainor, they hook us, and we sing their songs with heart.

My students are rowdy, but they're fun, and I don't mind the banter. I remember doing the same thing. I remember the pull of the melody of my favorite songs. I remember lingering over the lyrics, and today I understand that those songs got at something else I couldn't name, and in some strange way they helped me grow up.

It was summer and I'd been at a party, though I can't remember which year it was, or whether the party was big or small. Summer parties were usually larger because we could spill out into backyards, spread out along the lakeshore, or sneak into the woods—a patch of forest we were all warned under penalty of *everything* to never go into, so of course that's where we went.

I remember I was ambivalent about going. I had a summer job I needed to get up early for, I wasn't sure who would be there, and I probably didn't like what I was wearing.

There was a boy at the party, and I'm going to call him Cooper. Cooper was gorgeous and funny and loved the New York City skyline as much as I loved Chicago's. He'd moved a couple of years before from Long Island and every conversation we'd have somehow touched on which set of skyscrapers was better. I was always teasing when I discussed the majestic merits of the Sears Tower or the John Hancock. Cooper, on the other hand, spoke with a homesick hauntedness I'd never understand until I moved away and the skyline was no longer a backdrop to my stage, the El no longer a pulse coursing through my bloodstream.

On this night, Cooper and I were listening to "Hook" by Blues Traveler, on repeat trying to memorize the lyrics. Specifically, when John Popper sort of sings, sort of raps.

Cooper and I dated once, but it was short-lived. He ended it. He made it heartbreakingly clear that it was all about the chase with me. It stung, but he was right; the two of us were buddies who were attracted to each other, but also got bored, fast. As long as we were friends, we both knew we could break the rules, and *that*, like watching the Chicago skyline turn to stars at night, was exciting.

The lyrics Cooper and I were memorizing made me sort of sad. I didn't trust the narrator. Was he writing because he had a passion to write, or was he just out to make a buck? In the song he admits that it makes no difference what he sings about as long as he sounds earnest, passionate. Like Cooper and me, he's established the rules. Except he acknowledges how tantalizing the pull is to break those rules. What's more, nobody will truly know if he's telling the truth or not. John Popper, the lead singer of Blues Traveler, brings up Peter Pan and tells us that even though he might've loved Wendy, nothing deeper could be established between the two of them because the hunt for Hook—any hook, anything with the suspense of sting and adventure and unknown—was too strong. Peter would never grow up.

And so it goes with Juliet on the night she meets and realizes who Romeo is—someone she's been told is no good for her. Someone she knows she ought to stay away from.

I don't doubt that Romeo and Juliet were attracted to each other, but sometimes I wonder if that attraction deepened because they were supposed to stay away from each other. I can't think of something more tantalizing than having a rule set, and wondering how it is I can break that rule.

Juliet steps out onto her balcony and sighs those famous words: "O Romeo, Romeo, wherefore art thou Romeo?/Deny thy father and refuse thy name."

She's been hooked. Romeo, who also knows the rules, has been hooked, too. Hiding in the bushes, listening to Juliet sigh his name and request that he deny who he is, he is undone: "Call me but love, and I'll be newly baptis'd;/Henceforth I never will be Romeo."

We watch the balcony scene in my class, and the girls gasp in delighted frenzy when Romeo climbs the wall to get to Juliet. I smile shyly, remembering my best friend Celena's balcony that opened from her room and the summer nights when, technically, we weren't breaking rules because we'd met curfew. Except that wasn't all we met.

It's all been done before, girls, is what I think to say, but I don't because while this is true, while this story of a boy and girl feeling a crush and wondering if it's love has happened a million times, to try to tone those feelings down, to try to make it sound like it's not a big deal, is like saying, "Don't scream on this rollercoaster." Or, "Those contractions aren't that bad."

Because while I think it would've behooved Peter Pan to mature (just a little bit), and see the magic in a love that doesn't have to be hunted after, I also think that love ought to begin with a little bit of restlessness, a little bit of mischief, a little tug of a hook that brings you back, a million times.

After we've read Act 2, Scene 2 out loud, and thoroughly wallowed in Romeo and Juliet's evening, I have my students analyze this scene.

They are to take on the persona of Romeo or Juliet and write a letter or journal entry about what just happened. They're to include details of the night: What was the weather like? What did the party sound like? What did they eat? What was it like when they first saw the other person? I want each to express both the dilemma they face as well as the love they feel. It's an exercise in tension, in urgency. If they can do this, if they can get lost in fiction, I believe they will dig up truth that they can hold on to when the time is right (or ripe, as the case may be), and they experience this love themselves.

The other activity I have my students complete comes from *Shakespeare Set Free*. They are to create a promptbook, a setting for this scene. It doesn't have to be a balcony in an Italian village. They could place this scene in Africa, in New York City, in the Rocky Mountains. The point is, the story can happen anywhere.

The students play with the language by marking up the scene with stage directions. We learn about center stage, upper right stage, etc. Where will Romeo stand when he gasps, "It is my lady, O it is my love:/O that she knew she were!" and breaks from iambic pentameter? How will he say this? What will he do with his hands? Should the language change if they're in the South, or the Bronx, or at Hogwarts?

By manipulating the scene, students have another chance to understand the story, and each time reading, watching, discussing, writing, and directing, the hook deepens, the story becoming a part of them, and them a part of the story.

~

The night of the party, the cicadas were out. I drove home with the radio off and the windows down so I could hear them. I've never been a fan of bugs, but these critters intrigued me. I loved looking at the shells they left on my backyard fence once they molted and flew into adulthood. The old skin was like tissue but completely unchanged from the shape of the cicada's body. It would be no problem to crush, but something about that made me sad; like whatever left it took care not to shatter what once held it. It was just a shell, but I wanted to protect it. Or, at the least, let it dissolve on its own.

I parked the car in the garage, but walked around to the front steps to sit. I wanted to listen to the cicadas for a while. I wanted to listen to the slowing rickety *whoosh rush* of the El. I wanted to watch the wind rustling the maple leaves overhead. I wanted to think about Cooper and the rules we'd set, and I wanted to think about the lyrics to "Hook." I knew them all, but I wanted to understand them.

Cooper sauntered up the sidewalk then. He tended to do that on nights we'd hung out together. He'd been thrilled, and he was ready to break the rules. I studied him as he walked toward me, hands in his pockets, smiling, tall, tan.

The cicadas sung sleepily overhead as we talked.

"You look nice tonight," Cooper said, leaning back on his hands.

I smiled. "Thank you," I said, not looking at him.

He nudged me with his knee, and I looked at him. "I've had fun with you," he said.

I remember now this was the summer I would be a sophomore in college. In a few months, my teen years would end.

Both of us were weeks away from beginning a new college year in different states, and I was weeks away from meeting the boy who would be my husband. When Cooper said he had fun with me, he meant it as a parting statement. We were saying goodbye to Neverland, and that was okay. I'd had fun with him, too, but we were molting. We were ready to take off, ready to grow up.

I walk around the room, watching my students work on their journal entries and promptbooks, and I think about Cooper, and "Hook," and Romeo, and Juliet. I wish it had ended differently for those two. They had a lovely, mischievous dance. They spoke poetry to each other that they *felt* more than they understood, but they never had a chance to fly, to sing a more nuanced and difficult melody, just as beautiful. They missed a chance to leave those shells clinging to the backyard fence, holding the shape of what was, while the body moved somewhere else.

9

Tricks

Hadley and I are in the car, driving home from a cancelled soccer practice. Thunder rumbles behind us, chasing us.

"Let's see if we can get home before any rain reaches the windshield," I say, keeping my voice light. This elder daughter of mine gets nervous in thunderstorms.

"Okay," she mumbles, her eyes fixed outside, her arms on either side of her body, braced against the seat of the car.

When practice began, the sun was out. The air felt heavy and there were clouds in the sky, but the weather didn't seem threatening. If there was a storm, it wasn't awake yet—perhaps just rustling the air a bit as one does turning over in bed, and the sheets shift ever so slightly. It was no threat.

I decided to go for a run while Hadley practiced, and so as she made her way onto the field, I stuck in my earbuds, put on my Meghan Trainor and Pitbull mix, and took off. Forty-five minutes into my run, my phone rang. Lightning was spotted, and practice was cancelled.

Once we were back in the car, Hadley told me she was afraid.

"You were safe," I told her, while slipping and sliding on the seat and fiddling with my keys; I'd had no time to cool down, and my limbs were dripping with sweat. "Your coach did the right thing bringing you to the barn," I said, breathlessly. The team practices at Concordia University, next to this great big barn marked *Cardinals* in red letters—the team mascot.

"I was afraid for you," Hadley said, studying the barn. "I didn't know if you had anywhere to go."

When Hadley was first born, a cardinal would bang itself on our sunroom window every morning. Over and over, it'd fly off a nearby tree branch and knock itself square in the face. We were nervous he was going to hurt himself, so we taped newspaper to the windows to prevent him from seeing himself and believing he was a threat.

Long after Hadley was walking and talking, someone told me that the presence of cardinals meant protection. Someone was thinking about us, and so a cardinal was sent, his red breast like fire and strength against the barren tree branches.

"There were cardinals all over," I told Hadley. "I was fine."

She knows the legend, but I could tell she wasn't satisfied with my answer. I turned around to face her and put my sweaty palm on her knee. "We're okay," I said, and Hadley nodded.

Thunder rumbled and she said, "Go," so I turned the key, put the car in reverse, then made my way off the dirt road, the wheels crunching the brown-red dirt and the birds—sparrows, robins, and indeed, cardinals—flew away as Hadley and I moved forward with the storm.

Now Hadley shifts restlessly and her brow furrows because we're stopped at a red light. I think of something to discuss to take her mind off what's consuming her.

"Are you excited for 5th grade?"

She tells me she is and then proceeds to tell me she's not

sure which teacher she hopes to get. One teacher has exercise balls for classroom seats. Another never turns the lights on and instead strings twinkle lights so they hang from the walls and ceiling. Still another has couches and a coffee table in her classroom.

"I had a coffee table in my classroom," I say.

"When you taught 5th grade?" Hadley asks.

"Yup. Well, 5th/6th grade split. It was my first year and I had each student decorate a piece of paper with their name on it, and we Mod Podged® it onto the table."

I tell Hadley I brought a couple of oversized chairs and set them up in the corner with the coffee table. "Sometimes we had Juicy Talks in that space," I say.

"Juicy Talks?"

"Yeah. You know, it's a play on words. I'd bring juice and usually a snack, and we'd discuss a topic that was a little controversial, or challenging. You know, a juicy topic."

We drive for a while. We are at the edge of a storm, the grey swamp of a cloud swallowing the sunshine whole. The sun will burn the cloud, and the cloud will cry out—lightning and thunder—and the rain will begin.

"The one thing I'm nervous about," Hadley tells me, "is having to learn Health from a boy teacher."

Of course, 5th grade is the grade when students get "the talk." I remember it well, both my own experience, and in my teaching. It is an awkward rite of passage. Our changing bodies, feelings that heat our cheeks, and the wonder of it all is a recipe for a nice slice of awkward pie.

It's the stuff of great stories, too. Surely, Hadley's 5th grade teachers understand this juggling of the awkward and the wonderful and that's why they've designed their rooms as such. Hadley and her classmates are at the edge of an electric tempest and this time of life calls for all the cardinals we can summon.

I think teachers of tweens and adolescents have a special and important job of pointing out beauty in this confusing and wondrous time. We can be the cardinals, which is what I think Shakespeare is doing when he introduces Friar Lawrence in Act 2, Scene 3 of *Romeo and Juliet*. We are at the point of the play when a shift is taking place. Romeo and Juliet are done fantasizing and are ready to realize what they've imagined. Romeo's on his way to discuss matters of matrimony with the Friar, but before we watch the two converse, the Friar is alone on stage discussing herbs:

> The grey-eyed morn smiles on the frowning night,
> Chequering the eastern clouds with streaks of light;
> And flecked darkness like a drunkard reels
> From forth day's path and Titan's fiery wheels:
> Now, ere the sun advance his burning eye,
> The day to cheer and night's dank dew to dry,
> I must up-fill this osier cage of ours
> With baleful weeds and precious-juiced flowers.
> The earth that's nature's mother is her tomb;
> What is her burying grave that is her womb,
> And from her womb children of divers kind
> We sucking on her natural bosom find,
> Many for many virtues excellent,
> None but for some and yet all different.
> O, mickle is the powerful grace that lies

In plants, herbs, stones, and their true qualities:
For nought so vile that on the earth doth live,
But to the earth some special good doth give,
Nor aught so good but strain'd from that fair use
Revolts from true birth, stumbling on abuse:
Virtue itself turns vice, being misapplied;
And vice sometimes by action dignified.

Almost every line boasts a language trick. This is a man who is careful with his words.

I pass out the soliloquy to my students, and, with the help of *Shakespeare Set Free*, we go over each line, identifying the tricks Shakespeare uses. Then, we try our hands at making our own language tricks. I have them write a few sentences, about anything, and use what they wrote to create personification, simile, allusions or metaphors.

At this point in our study, I want my students to try to read the play for themselves, so I divide the class into groups, and have them make a museum exhibit for the different scenes in Act 2. With butcher paper, the groups draw Friar Lawrence and Romeo talking, Romeo messing around with Benvolio and Mercutio, and the Nurse teasing Juliet until she finally says, *yes*, Juliet will be Romeo's wife shortly. They write a little summary of each scene, along with any language tricks they find as they read. The scenes move quickly, and this exercise is like a sports drill—practicing a jump shot, a fastball, a serve before playing the game.

I want my students to really interact with the language and get to know these language tricks so they can use them in their own writing. It's like working on a puzzle, and then eventually creating your own, and I think this kind of deep thinking and creative work helps students to not so much run away from the tempest, but stand in it for a bit.

Because, after this, the stars begin to cross, and lightning is no longer a strobe in the clouds, but a pulsing vein searching to strike and electrify. Cardinals sent to protect can make fatal mistakes, and children are left on the open field to play the game for themselves.

10

Polka-Dotted Sneakers

The shoes were knock-off Keds®. Black, with white polka dots. Super comfortable, and versatile, too. They looked cute with skirts, pencil pants, jeans, maxi-dresses, shorts, and perhaps best, they added a pop of whimsy and independence to a school uniform. I noticed this charming fact when a student of mine, who I'll call *Radley*, was wearing the shoes the same day I was wearing mine.

"Nice taste," I said to Radley as I passed out the board-work for that day.

She and I giggled for a minute, but I wasn't sure she wanted me to draw too much attention to the fact that her teacher was wearing the same shoes she was.

Radley had long, brown, beach-wavy hair and brown eyes. Head bowed, she'd peek shyly through her hair. She was quiet, and except for her hair, which was way better than mine, Radley reminded me of fourteen-year-old Callie. Even her academic profile matched. I could tell she was observant and thoughtful because her writing was descriptive and articulate, but there was never enough of it. Radley often turned in half-completed assignments that started strong but petered out towards the middle. Often, she didn't turn in anything at all.

I knew this wasn't due to a lack of intelligence. Like four-teen-year-old Callie, who covered her English folder with

Deee-Lite and U2 song lyrics, *Do The Right Thing* and *Princess Bride* quotes, and oodles of hearts with boys' names written inside them, Radley had a lot going on in her mind. I can vividly remember learning about writing a bibliography for our research paper in Mr. Gates' 8th grade English class (mine was on thalidomide, a topic I'd chosen from the hit song "We Didn't Start the Fire," by Billy Joel), while at the same time staring at Neal's shiny-blond hair.

I knew Radley was interested in the material we discussed in class; it was just that she was equally interested in other things. It's like going to Target knowing you're there for toilet paper, knowing toilet paper is the right and important choice to make, but you see the most adorable pair of black sneakers with white polka dots and you think, "What did I come in here for again?"

Radley once wrote about the band One Direction. It was the longest paper I'd read from her. We were studying creative nonfiction, and at the end of the unit, I asked the class to choose one piece they had been working on to revise and submit.

"Choose something that's risky," I told them. "Choose a piece that makes you nervous, or afraid, or sad to take a look at again." I wanted my students to see what they could create with what made them uncomfortable. Radley chose to write about the boy band One Direction.

She had five friends, just like the band, and together they listened to the boys' songs, discussed the lyrics, posted band pictures to their bedroom walls and notebooks, and bonded over their shared adoration for Louis, Niall, Liam, Harry, and Zayn.

Everything was great until the girls began to disagree over who loved and knew which band member better. There were freeze-outs, passive-aggressive social media insults, and soon, this friendship dissolved, right around the time the band broke up.

I felt like I was reading one of my journal entries from 8th grade, which, by the way, I still have. When I go back to read them, after I stop cringing, I think, "What else, Callie? I know more was going on. I remember. Why didn't you write anything else?"

What do we do to bring more out of teenagers? How do we merge the need for toilet paper with the feelings we have for black sneakers with polka dots?

A few weeks after she turned in her One Direction essay, Radley performed a scene from *Romeo and Juliet* with her friend Lea. Radley played Juliet, and Lea was the Nurse. They performed the scene where the Nurse playfully stalls as Juliet begs her to say what she's learned after speaking to Romeo. Will Romeo and Juliet be married or not?

Lea was hilarious, and I was thoroughly entertained but not surprised. Her sarcasm and wit paired well with the Nurse's role in this scene.

"I am a-weary," she said, limping on stage, fake gasping for breath. She had a hand on her lower back as she walked. "Give me leave a while." Lea plopped herself on a makeshift bed they set up to pretend they were in Juliet's bedroom.

"Nay, come, I pray thee speak, good, good, Nurse." Radley kneeled next to the bed, pleading with Lea, who was moaning and rubbing her feet.

"Do you not see that I am out of breath?" Lea asked.

Radley shot up to her feet. A few of her classmates flinched and sat up straighter. "Whoa," one of them said, and I admit, I was thinking the same thing. I'd never seen Radley this bold before.

"How are thou out of breath," Radley demanded, "when thou has breath/To say to me that thou are out of breath?" Radley annunciated *breath* and hearing it said this way, her classmates and I laughed, catching the taunting sarcasm.

"It's a good point," one of her classmates whispered.

Radley put her hands on her hips, looked at us, and began to speak. "The excuse that thou dost make in this delay/ is longer than the tale thou dost excuse." She'd brought us into the conversation and we laughed again, delighted to be in on the aside. Radley's decision to deliver the line this way was a perfectly placed teenage thing to do.

I continued to watch as Radley spun around and leapt on stage, chasing after the Nurse, trying to get information from her. Radley's hair flew and twirled. A confidence I'd never seen from her came through that day. My seemingly timid student had completely transformed.

I think this is because Radley understood how Juliet felt. She knew that strange desperation of loving a person (albeit one she barely knew), and wanting so badly for that person to love her back. I believe she was drawing from her own life, and she could do that because Juliet provided words for how she feels. Watching Radley, I thought of her One Direction essay, and realized she was not only trying to express the love she had for a band whose music captured her heart, but she was also exploring the heartbreak of that band breaking up, and the loss of a childhood friendship.

Maybe I should've taught *Romeo and Juliet* before my class wrote creative nonfiction. I could've told Radley, "Do what you did with Act 2, Scene 5 when you revise. Pull Juliet out." I hope though, now that Radley has grappled with Shakespeare's language, now that she's met Juliet, she can pull Juliet out of herself.

We studied *To Kill a Mockingbird* as well that year, and Radley struggled with it at the beginning of the story. She wrote a note on one of her unfinished assignments, telling me she was having a hard time getting into it. I told her to stick around for a few minutes after class so we could talk more.

"The beginning is really hard," I told her. I remember complaining to my mom that it was like reading the Old Testament with all those Finches all over the place. "Who cares? Get to the point!" I might've yelled.

I told Radley to watch the movie first. "You'll have a good sense of the plot, and then reading it won't be so overwhelming."

Radley smiled shyly and said, "No teacher has ever said watch the movie first."

I smiled, and looked at the floor, feeling a little insecure about my own academic struggles as a student, unsure of how much to say.

I thought of those polka-dotted shoes she and I both had, and the day I found them in Target. I wasn't supposed to be in the shoe aisle. I was there for toilet paper, but I'd forgotten about it once I saw those shoes.

"Well," I said to Radley, "it's what I did when I was fourteen." I started walking to my desk. "And I turned out all right." I laughed.

"So I can find it on Netflix?" she asked.

"I'm sure you can," I said as I began to sort through papers on my desk.

Radley started for the door.

"Look out for Boo Radley," I said to her. "He's full of surprises."

I sat down at my desk, picked up a red pen, and uncapped it, ready to make a mark. *Just like you, Radley.*

11

At the Door

It was a Friday night sometime in the spring of my senior year of high school, when my friends and I thought it would be hilarious to see how many boys we could get to ask us to the prom. Nobody was off limits; however, no kissing or any fooling around of that sort could commence. We could promise the boys nothing. We were to use only the power of flirtation to evoke images of slipping corsages onto our wrists, a warm spring evening walking along Michigan Avenue in a tuxedo with a pretty gal in a sparkly spaghetti-strapped dress alongside, ready to dance the night away.

I remember sitting around a kitchen table with a group of friends shortly after we'd established the challenge. A recently shaved swimmer (state championship season was upon us)—his blue eyes and black lashes striking in contrast with his bald head—nudged me in the side playfully with his elbow. I turned toward him slowly, eyebrows raised. He glided his hand across my back and cupped my shoulder so I'd lean close, and he whispered, "Do you have a prom date?"

"Not yet," I whispered back.

Game on.

I was not in my part of the neighborhood, the South side of Oak Park. That's the side with the El and Gina's Italian Ice, Rehm Park and the Oak Park Bakery where, on Saturdays, I'd

go with my dad and the ladies there would give me two but-
tery sugar cookies coated with rainbow sprinkles tucked nicely
into a pink wax paper bag. The ladies didn't give me cookies
anymore. I was usually asleep when my dad walked to the bakery by himself to get Saturday morning treats.

I was not with Celena, either. I'm sure we'd seen each
other at one point that night, but this group of girls, this side
of town, was different. The girls were fun and funny, but
among them was an underlying current of concern for what
everyone else was doing, saying, wearing, and it all went back
to how they measured up. Celena never played that game, and
I don't remember why we weren't together that night, but I
do remember understanding that our time together—seeing
each other every day, calling each other last thing before bed
every night, laughing so hard together and knowing what
mood the other was in by the way she walked, was coming to
an end. In a few months, she'd go to the University of Wiscon-
sin, and I was supposed to go to Bethel College, but I didn't want
to go, and hadn't told my parents that yet.

I didn't know what I wanted, and these people, this side of
town, were all new. It felt like an escape—a break from real-
ity. I didn't want to deal with growing up, leaving home, parting with Celena, so I played Project Confuse-a-Boy instead.

At one point during the night, we went to a diner called
Gossage Grill, a popular joint for teenagers. This was the first
and only time I'd been there and I can remember being
charmed by the greasy corner restaurant with waiters who
wore white paper hats and guys sitting at the steel counter
drinking coffee and eating burgers. I also remember feeling
sad because what I looked at reminded me of the painting,

Boulevard of Broken Dreams where Elvis Presley, Humphrey Bogart, and Marilyn Monroe sit around the table. I remember seeing that painting in a storefront, and I remember my mom telling me it was a replica of another painting called *Nighthawks*. The one with the dead pop icons made me sad. What were they talking about? How were they doing? Were they happy?

Because of the way Gossage Grill was set up, it was easy to park a car, leave the radio on, and have a dance party while you waited for your fries and soda. I loved a dance party (still do), and this is my second and only other memory of Gossage Grill. I was dancing, and then I stopped to say hello to two classmates, Kristin and Jennie. I do not remember what we said to each other or why we spoke in the first place. I didn't know either of them too well, and it wasn't like me to walk up and say hello, but the night had an urgency to it: I was feeling bold, or maybe I felt dangerous. I couldn't tell the difference. I was winning the prom game. I was losing myself. I was scared.

I remember Kristin's smile, and being happy to talk with her. I remember it was dark save for the lights from the cars and the diner. I remember the smell of burgers and fries, gas from running motors, and the factories from Gary, Indiana, their smells drifting across Lake Michigan. I knew spring was here to stay when I could smell those factories. I remember my back was to the floor-to-ceiling window where the old men sat, and Kristin and Jennie faced the diner, as though they were going to order.

The next morning, I was in a step aerobics class at a neighborhood gym. The past four years, Saturdays were spent practicing Drill Team routines and that was over, too, so I signed up at a gym to take aerobics. It wasn't to stay in shape. I knew myself the most, or I was most comfortable with myself, dancing to a pulsing, synchronized beat and I was afraid I had to say goodbye to that, too. Those Saturday aerobics classes felt more like a battle to hang onto something that was already gone.

I took two classes on Saturdays, and in between them, while getting a drink at the water fountain, I found out Kristin and Jennie were dead. It was a double suicide. They'd left a note on the kitchen table.

What follows next are fragments. News crews staked out at our high school. Classes cancelled so we could attend funerals. Jennie's father standing at the pulpit in a church on Oak Park Avenue, wearing grey slacks and a blue button-down shirt, barely speaking in sentences.

One morning shortly after this happened, I stood in the doorway of our bathroom off the kitchen downstairs, watching my mom pluck her eyebrows, her hips against the bathroom sink, her neck long, reaching toward her reflection. She was beautiful and strong. I knew I'd put her through a lot those last months of high school, and probably there'd be more to come, but that morning I needed to say two things.

"Mom," I began, and she *mmm-hmmed* quietly while she plucked.

"I promise I won't ever do what Kristin and Jennie did," I said, and I leaned against the doorframe when I said it.

My mom dropped her arms, and the tweezer quietly clanked on the sink. She turned to look at me. "Thank you," she breathed, and I have never heard such relief in her voice. It hadn't occurred to me that she was scared.

"Also, I don't think I want to go to Bethel College," I said.

My mom barely flinched. "Okay," she said, calmly, still looking at me.

"I don't know why," I continued and started to cry, "I'm scared."

"It's scary," she said, and she stayed where she was, facing me with one hand on the sink. I shifted my weight so I could lean on the other side of the threshold, and that's what I remember: the two of us, standing in the morning light, together scared.

This is not a story I tell my students, though it is an event I think of when we get to the scene when Mercutio and Tybalt die, specifically, my memory of those few minutes with Kristin and Jennie at Gossage Grill. What could've become of them? What could've become of Elvis? Of Marilyn Monroe? What about Mercutio and Tybalt? What could they have become? Where did everything go wrong?

There is so much to mourn in Act 3, Scene 1: the loss of a hilarious, boisterous young man (even at his death, he is joking, "Ay, Ay, a scratch, a scratch"); the loss of a protective cousin; the fact that these boys allowed temper to get the best of them; Romeo's banishment from Verona after just getting married; the breakup of a boyhood friendship forever.

We are now stepping into teenage tragedy, and this, sadly, is only the beginning. What's tragic is certainly the anger and the prejudice that are present throughout this play, but equally so is the fact that teenagers feel and experience things that they don't always know how to handle or articulate. If we are going to teach this play, it is good to point out how anger motivates action, but it is also important to mourn. If we only point out the wrong these boys did, we are ignoring a part of the teenager that is conflicted about these characters. We ignore the brother who walks his younger sister to class to make sure that slick-looking boy knows who he's trying to flirt with. Her brother knows what it feels like to be protective. No, he'd never kill, but he'd make sure nobody hurt his little sister, either.

We ignore the student who has a comeback for everything, who drapes his limbs on his desk and slips his feet underneath his peers' chairs, never sitting up straight, never taking anything seriously, but who asks, "Where's Mercutio's dad? He needs a dad. He's like me. I don't know who my daddy is."

There's so much to sit with in this scene, so much to understand. It's been over 20 years since that night in 1994, and I still don't understand it. Each spring though, when I begin to feel a recklessness that I know now is a mixture of boldness and fear, bravery and anxiety, I refer to my 18-year-old self, and I walk through that night again. I always end standing a few feet away from my mom, telling her I am afraid.

So I think what I can offer my students when we read this scene is a chance to experience it. I don't throw out morals, and I don't point out who was in the wrong, or who started it. I help students understand the language, as in any part of the play. We watch clips of this scene to compare and contrast them. I walk them through this part of the story, and I make space for however they want to react. There are a lot of reactions and feelings in the classroom on this day, and while this might be more dramatic and intense, it's not much different than, say, any given day with 8th graders.

I have no idea who will walk through my classroom door when English begins. Someone could ask me if she has too much lipgloss on (usually, the answer is yes), or she could want advice on whether her metaphors work in an essay; he could be a superstar basketball player with a gal on either side of him at the beginning of class, but he stays after class, helping me straighten out the classroom and telling me about his upcoming 14th birthday party. "I hope people show up. I don't know if anyone will show up." There is so much to process, so much to articulate.

After we read this scene and discuss it, I have students write something called "Lazy Sonnets" that I learned about from *Shakespeare Set Free*. The poem is still 14 lines, and it follows the same rhyming pattern, but each line is only one word. Students use this method of poetry to summarize Act 3, Scene 1, but also to get at the intensity of the scene. Their words need to be specific, sharp, like daggers.

One year, I had a student who was a lot to handle. She would be wild one minute and desperately sad the next. I'd kicked her out of class before for belligerent behavior. Once, when she was writing, she stood and walked over to the wall to sniff it. The class laughed, and I made a move to do something about it, but she sat back down and wrote, so I left her alone. She wrote an essay in the second person about her uncle who used to work on drywall, but is now in jail. She wanted to get the smell of the classroom wall right. Every time she walks into a classroom and breathes in, she remembers him and feels a pinch.

She was particularly attached to Mercutio. She loved Mercutio, because, she told me, she related to him. "Not just the inappropriate stuff, Mrs. Feyen. I'm a good friend, like him."

"You are," I said.

On the day Mercutio died, she was the last to leave class. I was leaning on the doorframe, wishing my students well as they left.

"I can't believe Mercutio's dead," she said.

"I know," I said. "Me, too." I shifted a bit. She always made me nervous. I never felt I had control over our exchanges because I couldn't anticipate what would happen next.

"We'll never find out more about him," she said, slinging her backpack on a shoulder. "It's scary." She had tears in her eyes. She cried and she laughed so easily.

"It is scary," I said. We stood in the doorway for a second —both halfway in the classroom, and halfway out—and then I said, "I'll see you tomorrow."

And I did.

12

Meeting in the Dark

I once had an idea for what I thought would be a Young Adult novel. The setting was the front steps of a condominium in the Washington, D.C., area. There would be two main characters: a young mother and a teenaged girl. They'd meet on the steps at night.

The mother would be on the steps because her baby wasn't sleeping and she'd done everything she could to try to convince her babe that sleep is good, but to no avail. Her husband would say, "Take a break, get some fresh air." So she would.

The couple would have a small balcony off their two-bedroom condo, and she could sit out there, but she'd still hear her baby, she'd still hear her husband, *sh, sh, shh*-ing, and saying, "It's okay, it's okay." Though she'd love the gentle steadiness of his voice, she'd need a little more space on those nights, and so down the stairwell and outside to the front of their building she'd go.

The steps she'd sit on would be cement, not wooden like the ones her father built for the home she grew up in, and they'd still be warm from the day's sun, and there'd be trees swaying overhead and fireflies out, and sitting there she'd breathe a little deeper and remember sitting on her front steps as a teenager at the end of the night just before heading in. She'd love the fresh start of the morning, but night would hold a mysterious pull. She'd see things differently in the dark.

The teenaged girl would be on her way in from a night out. She'd see the woman on the steps as she walked up the sidewalk, and wish the woman wasn't there. The girl wanted those steps for herself. She wasn't ready to leave the night's embrace, but she sure didn't want to share it with someone's mom. Why would a mom be out anyway? Shouldn't she be folding laundry and watching TV or something? On this night, she'd brush past the mom, but eventually there'd be a time when the two would converge on the stairs and share some kind of awkward connection, but a connection just the same, because the girl would be in need.

I remembered this seed of a story the week I was preparing my lessons for Act 3, Scene 2 of *Romeo and Juliet*. At its beginning, Juliet is waiting, longingly, to consummate her marriage to Romeo: "bring in cloudy night immediately./Spread thy close curtain, love-performing Night,/That runaways' eyes may wink, lovers can see to do their amorous rites/..." However, Juliet's sensual reverie ends when she finds out from the Nurse what Romeo has done: "Tybalt is gone and Romeo banished,/Romeo that killed him, he is banished." I imagine the Nurse wailing, and then Juliet riffs a slew of the most pitch-perfect insults one could give to the boy she fell in love with: "beautiful tyrant, fiend angelical; damned saint, honourable villain…was ever book containing such vile matter/so fairly bound? O that deceit should dwell/In such a gorgeous palace!"

Romeo's not doing much better. He suggests stabbing himself to death, but the nurse grabs his dagger from him. It is Friar Lawrence, with his fifty-three-line rousing pep talk to Romeo, who sheds some light on a very dark night: "Take heed, take heed, for such die miserable./Go get thee to thy love as was decreed,/Ascend to her chamber, hence and comfort her;/But look thou stay not till the Watch be set,/For then thou can'st not pass to Mantua, To blaze your marriage, reconcile your friends,/Beg pardon of the prince,/and call thee back/With twenty hundred thousand times more joy/Than thou went'st forth in lamentation."

There is a lot to process in these scenes, a lot to tread through with the students who are the same age as Romeo and Juliet were, and I wasn't sure where to start. I felt a lot like the mama sitting on the steps one summer evening when her teenaged neighbor walks over and sits down, visibly upset. What should she do? What should she say that won't make things worse? I wonder sometimes if the teenaged years are a second sort of infancy, when everything is new again; everything shocks.

At the same time I was preparing these lessons, my younger daughter, Harper, had taken an interest in *Where the Wild Things Are*. Our before-bed routine consisted of reading a picture book, one picked by Hadley and one by Harper, plus a chapter from a novel. My girls usually picked the same story three or four nights in a row because they liked to study the story; each evening they asked different questions, saw something new about it. For Harper, it was Max and his wild things.

We'd discuss Max getting sent to his room, and I confessed that had happened to me, but I also whispered, "I kind of liked being sent to my room."

"You did?" Harper asked, her eyes wide.

"Well, yeah," I said with a sly smile. "It's where I was left alone to imagine a thing or two, like Max."

I'm sure neither my mom nor I realized this at the time, but reading Sendak's story, I thought what a nice thing my mother gave me when I was getting uppity: a place I was safe to let my imagination run wild.

We talked about Max being afraid of the beasts, too.

"But he thought them up," Harper said. "Why would he be afraid?"

"Have you ever been afraid of something you imagined?" I asked. "Maybe you've drawn something and you didn't realize it would be that real, that good?"

So what do we do when it's dark and we've created something we are afraid of? What do we do when we begin to understand something differently?

The first year I taught *Romeo and Juliet* was my first year teaching middle school after a ten-year break. It was also Harper's first year of school. The day she started kindergarten was also the day I zipped up my grey pencil skirt and slipped on a pair of heels for the first time in a decade. I felt a little like Max in his wolf costume. I was still a mommy, but I wasn't only a mommy. The thought scared and thrilled me at the same time. Seeing myself as Mrs. Feyen felt a little wild— like the woman sitting on those steps at night, remembering herself in the dark.

I decided I'd start my teaching with Max, and we'd explore *night* together.

When my students came to class, I told them to make a web with the word *night* in the center and add anything they thought of when they read that word. We spent time writing and illustrating poems about night, based on the webs we created.

Next, I read them *Where the Wild Things Are* and we looked carefully at night and Max's imagination (what it is he was able to do) and how that differed from Romeo and Juliet's situation. We also watched as Max's mother gave Max space to explore the dark, to get mischievous, and to know he could come home. Max could always come home. This was not the case with Romeo and Juliet.

Finally, we used prompts from *Shakespeare Set Free* and wrote a double journal entry, from either the perspective of the Nurse and Juliet or Friar Lawrence and Romeo. I wanted my students to write in the voice of these characters—an adult and a teenager—so they could see and struggle with both sides. And the students wrote and illustrated "Night" poems, an exercise in creating mystery. I wanted them to command a wild rumpus, and I wanted them to see things differently as they played with something they don't entirely understand but cannot look away from.

My hope for my Young Adult novel was that eventually the mother and the teenaged girl would talk on that stoop late at night. Through their shared storytelling, they'd see the world a little differently, they'd grow into who they were supposed to be through this exchange in the dark. I thought to call the book *Lotus Flowers* because these flowers grow in the mud. They cannot grow without darkness.

13

Set to Music

I was a senior in high school when I first heard the Indigo Girls' song "Ghost." It was winter, or it was going to be winter. I was cold. I remember that. My mom and I were driving around the Midwest, making college visits.

I was looking out the window at a dull, grey day listening to a mixtape my friend Lisa made for me. That's what we did back then for friends and boyfriends: put together a compilation of songs that we liked, or that had a memory attached, or that articulated something we were trying to say but didn't know how. Lisa loved the Indigo Girls, and every mixtape she made me had one of their songs on it. We both blame the song "Closer to Fine" on a ditched class or two.

I didn't know my passion for metaphor at the time, but I really liked the comparison the singers made to the Mississippi River's beginnings and that of love. Both start seemingly small, and perhaps powerless, like a stream we can walk across, but both have powerful currents that can wash us out to sea. This sort of love—or loss; I'm not sure what it was—was sad, but hearing that sadness phrased this way was somehow relieving to me. "Ghost" felt like a balm and I listened to it over and over again on a red Walkman during that college visit.

About ten or eleven months prior to the college visits, I'd met a boy. He was in my geology class, though I'd known who he was before that. I remember seeing him in the hallway once with his letterman jacket and his spiky blond hair (I was such a sucker for spiky, messed-up hair). He had blue eyes and incredibly rosy cheeks and even though he didn't say a word to me—he didn't even look at me that day in the hallway—he was that tributary I could be delighted by, but doubted it'd ever come to anything. His name was Thomas.

Except he did become something—something more than I was ready to handle—and in August he left for college.

The day before Thomas left, he did the valiant thing and broke it off with me. He didn't want to do it, and I didn't want him to do it, which made the breakup devastating. It also made it difficult to not communicate with each other. I was a year away from getting my first email account, so in those days, I'd rush home from school hoping to find a handwritten letter from Thomas. Some days I would, and the grey-blue stationery that I thought matched his eyes, and his untidy cursive, would send me into an exhilarated state and then a funk so low not even Drill Team could lighten me up.

I didn't understand what was going on or what I was going through, but it felt serious. It wasn't fun and mysteriously enchanting like it was with the other boys I'd hung out with. It was dark and sad.

I remember one day I was in my expository writing class, my favorite class at the time, when my teacher, Mr. Smith, asked me to stick around after class. This was par for me—I was a terrible student, and it took until the beginning of October for teachers to figure this out and get over their bafflement that they'd got their first impression wrong. (I was quiet, organized, had impeccable handwriting, was the captain of the Drill Team, and I dressed rather well. I had "good student" written all over me.)

I assumed this is what Mr. Smith was doing. We'd been working on our college application essays, and as my classmates filed out, I prepared myself for what I figured he wanted to say: Perhaps I should consider junior college. That way, I wouldn't have to concern myself with writing about why I wanted a higher education.

Instead, he wanted to talk to me about the necklace I was wearing. Thomas had sent it to me in a recent letter. It was gold with two Greek letters on it—his fraternity.

"You're lavaliered," Mr. Smith told me, and he said it as though he was at a funeral or was about to give the world's most difficult final exam.

"I guess," I said, tucking the necklace underneath my T-shirt.

"That's serious," he said. I looked at my Keds.

Then he told me my college essay was good, and I looked up, surprised. He told me in an equally cautious voice that I was a thoughtful writer, that he believed I had the ability to develop this skill if I worked at it, that probably a smaller school (and not the one Thomas was attending) would suit me better.

That was one of the reasons I was applying to smaller schools, and I told him that. I had no intention of going to a big state school.

"Okay," he said, and handed me back my essay—an A.

"Okay," I repeated, and left.

I stopped wearing Thomas's necklace in class, but I had it on in the car while my mom drove around looking at colleges while I listened to "Ghost" for what I'm sure was the billionth time that day.

Even then, I'm sure I would admit to being melodramatic, but when the Indigo Girls sang "Ghost," I swear I lost my breath. They named exactly how I felt.

This story is one of the reasons I take Romeo and Juliet so seriously. I've felt how Juliet's felt. Several times. I know my students have felt or will feel this way, too. Love, or whatever it is we're feeling, takes us by the ears (or chest, or heart) and tosses us around like ragdolls. We are both wrecked and hoping for more. It is the strangest beauty.

Romeo and Juliet is not just an old story that makes no difference anymore. Stories such as *Eleanor & Park*, *The Romeo and Juliet Code*, and *The Wednesday Wars* are modern tales that parallel the plot and themes of Shakespeare's tragedy. Often, the similarities might not even be a deliberate act of the story-teller. The same is true for songs, and I want my students to see that what is happening in fair Verona is also happening on their neighborhood streets, on the pages of the library books they pick out or even in the news they watch or read, and the social media they scroll through. Romeo and Juliet's story is heard through my students' earbuds as they listen to their Spotify mixes.

So we take a look at these songs and see if we can match the lyrics to a character's personality, or something he or she might say. I start class with a lyric matchup. I take excerpts from popular songs and I have students write who in *Romeo and Juliet* might say these words. It's a fun activity that gets us laughing, but also shows the students that not much has changed. We've been grappling with and making poetry out of love since time began.

In the next part of class, I introduce the "Songs and Stories" paper. This is a five-paragraph essay in which students are to choose one character in *Romeo and Juliet*, and match a song with him or her.

Despite this play's subject matter and the outcome, I want my students to play around with the story and draw parallels to other events, stories, and their own lives. I believe that by giving them this opportunity, I can help them layer themselves with stories. This is not to protect them from love; rather, it is so when love arrives—when that small tributary becomes a raging river—my students have something to hold on to.

14

Juliet Moment

On the day we were to read Juliet's soliloquy, where she expresses how afraid she is not only to take the poison, but also of what the ramifications will be, one of my 8th graders, Josh, walked into class with an oven mitt on his hand. I asked him why he was wearing an oven mitt and he told me that it hurt to open his binder, and that the mitt made it easier to open it. *Fair enough*, I thought, but then asked, "Hey, Josh, aren't you right-handed?" His mitt was on his right hand.

"I'm right-handed, yes."

"How will you write in class today?" I asked.

"I can do it."

I had the class write about a time when they were really scared—so scared that they couldn't control their thoughts. I wanted them to relate to how Juliet must've felt when she gave her soliloquy before she took the poison. They wrote and they wrote and it was so quiet I got a little nervous.

"Now, look what you wrote," I said, "and see if there is anything else on the page besides fear."

Lots of them found things like anger, confusion, sadness, and that all made a lot of sense. It's what I assumed they'd find.

Well, Josh, he found something different. He raised his oven-mitted hand and told us that one time he thought there was a stranger in the house. He told us he got out of bed and went to find the stranger in order to save his parents from him or her.

"I was scared," Josh said, "but what got me out of the bed was the love I have for my parents. So I see love in what I wrote."

I feel so sorry for Juliet in this scene where she's deciding to take the poison. It is difficult for me to read, "I have a faint cold fear thrills through my veins/That almost freezes up the heat of life:/I'll call them [the Nurse and her mother] back again to comfort me./"Nurse! What should she do here?/My dismal scene I needs must act alone."

I have my fair share of times when I've been so scared I've called for my mom, my cries instinctual. Running from a loose dog, being homesick at camp, hearing a best friend tell me she hates me. "Mommy." "Mama." "Mom." Her name might've changed slightly, but the call was the same: "Help me! What do I do?"

Yet, this is the point when Juliet changes from a docile daughter to the heroine of the play. It is not just in the act of drinking from the vial and taking this into her own hands; it is in looking at, and naming, her fears—alone—that she shows her gumption. "Act 4 belongs to Juliet," writes Peggy O'Brien in *Shakespeare Set Free*. "It is in this scene that Juliet resolves to drink the potion that will take her close to death, and she draws the audience to her as she speaks her desperate fears aloud. Here she tells the truth as she knows it and reveals her own painful internal conflict."

We take a look at what it is Juliet fears: that the potion the Friar gave her is actually meant to kill her; or that she won't die, but instead Romeo won't find her and she'll be locked in the family tomb forever; that, being locked in the tomb, she'll lose her mind and use Tybalt's bones to "dash out [her] desperate brains."

Shakespeare Set Free suggests the students create the tomb Juliet describes using an empty shoebox, and we spent a couple of class days creating mandrakes and skeletons out of construction paper. It is unnerving to take a close look at fear. The lesson is a rather gruesome one, but when Josh pointed out that he saw love alongside his fear, I think he was onto something.

We could read Juliet's soliloquy and roll our eyes at her melodrama. We could decide this is all much ado about nothing, and, in fact, some students do say Juliet should trust that her parents know what they're doing insisting on her marrying Paris.

Or we can be more like Josh and Juliet. That is, we can look closely at and wonder about our fear, but understand we must move forward because we believe something greater and stronger than what we're afraid of lies within us.

Because of the ending, it is tempting to turn this tragedy into several "warning lessons" or even a guide for how teenagers (and parents) shouldn't behave. I don't think reading is much fun (or worthwhile) when we look at literature this way. Instead, I try to look for "me too" moments that I can share with my students in the hopes they can learn that it is normal to be afraid, to be shocked by love, to be angry.

Though I only say one word, this is my "Juliet Moment." My parents and I were standing behind my dorm on a late August afternoon. I was officially a freshman in college except for one thing: I had to say goodbye to my mom and dad.

Goodbye had been lurking all day. I'd seen it in the cardboard boxes I was emptying of wool socks and jeans, watched it roll around the fitted sheet my mom shook out before she tucked it snugly on my mattress corners. It taunted me like a bully smirking in the corner while my dad put Diet Cokes and apples in the mini fridge he'd bought for me. *Goodbye* was eagerly waiting to swallow me whole. Or maybe it would torture me and take nibbles of my toes and fingers, saving my heart for last.

The three of us stood facing each other, and the leaves on the trees overhead hung heavy in the August heat.

"Okay," my mom said and I wasn't surprised at the strength I heard in her voice. She was always the band-aid-ripper-offer. It was my dad who prompted what I did next. His eyes watered and his lip trembled and I knew if I stayed there so much as ten more seconds, I'd never go to college.

I bolted.

"Bye!" I said, hugging them both, but barely. I couldn't afford to have their arms linger around me. I stepped back, pivoted, and ran. I flung open the door to my building, and took the stairs two at a time. Once I got to my room, I slammed that door, and locked it. I sat down on a small white couch my Aunt Lucy gave me—a portion of a giant sectional she kept in her living room and that the kids were never allowed on—and willed myself not to cry.

A giant mosquito buzzed its way up and down my wall. Startled, I watched it and panicked. My dad always took care of these things.

I put my hands on my knees, rose, walked to the wall, took off one of my sneakers, and whacked that bug to its death. Then, I unrolled a Luke Perry (a.k.a. Dylan McKay) poster and taped it on the wall where I'd killed the bug.

The rest of the afternoon, I sharpened pencils and put them in my Chicago Cubs plastic cup. I folded sweaters and stacked them in my closet. I plugged in my radio and TV. I put pictures of my family and friends on my desk and bookshelves.

It wasn't deciding whether or not to drink a potion that would fake my death, but I know about fear. I know how it feels to be lost. I understand wanting to call for mom and dad with every ounce of my soul. I also know how it feels to decide I can be afraid, but I can move forward.

I don't want my students to have to face exactly what Juliet faces, but I know they'll have times when they are afraid, so afraid their imagination gets away from them. I want them to name what they feel, as Juliet did. And like Juliet, move forward with fierceness and gumption. Oven mitts or not.

15

Go Hence

My husband Jesse was the first person to tell me that I dodge conflict in my writing. He said it shortly after he'd read a story I wrote about a girl and her friends spending an afternoon at the pool. I was most proud of the scene where the group of friends had a fireball contest during the rest period. The object was to see who could keep the Red Hots jawbreaker in her mouth the longest. One girl, Molly, continually snapped the straps of her bathing suit so they slapped her shoulders, in order to keep the fireball in her mouth, because she'd heard it's impossible for two parts of your body to be in pain at the same time.

Jesse told me my description was fantastic. I'd made the setting Oak Park, Illinois, the town I grew up in, and he said he could hear the El, see the Sears Tower, and smell the chlorine in the pool.

"But," he said, "nothing happens."

"What do you MEAN nothing happens?" I said, grabbing my beloved story from his hands.

"There's no conflict," he tried to explain.

"What you do MEAN, 'There's no conflict'?" I demanded. "Did you not read the fireball scene?"

Hadley, who was just shy of 18 months at the time, and so close to walking, was eating Cheerios® as she waddled around the coffee table, one hand keeping her steady. Jesse had strategically placed the cereal inches away from each other in the hopes she'd take steps to get to the little O's.

"That's a great scene," he told me, placing more Cheerios for Hadley on the coffee table, "but that's not really conflict. It's more like action." He threw a Cheerio in the air and caught it in his mouth. "Or comedy." I rolled my eyes and watched Hadley.

She was so good at grabbing the Cheerios. She never reached or dropped to the ground to crawl to the next one. I could tell her hand on the coffee table was only there for security, and not for balance. I felt like there were only minutes before she'd let go, and step into official toddlerhood.

The coffee table Hadley moved around was a gift from my parents. It replaced an IKEA one Jesse and I had stained blue, and I had cut magazines to make a collage on the table's legs. The coffee table my parents bought us was beautiful—sturdy, with thick wooden legs and a slate top. Jesse and I loved it, but I felt a tug saying goodbye to the other one we'd spent a Sunday afternoon staining and decorating. It was an Easter Sunday, and I'd had a cold, and in church that morning while holding the grape juice cup for communion, I'd sneezed, broken the cup, and splattered its contents all over me. I never take communion now without thinking of that day, but I also remember being outside with Jesse on a barely-there spring day, working on our $40 coffee table.

I picked our new coffee table out with my dad one day. "This is the one I want," I told him. *And he bought it*, I thought, while I watched Jesse help his little girl get where she wanted to go. Once Hadley figured out what she could do, there would be no going back.

"You're a placeholder," Jesse said, breaking me out of my reverie.

"Huh?"

"You've set up a beautiful space for these girls. But now what? What do they do in it?"

"They have a fireball contest," I stubbornly insisted, but I knew what he meant. Something had to happen.

Conflict, like verb tense shifts and when to use a comma, has always been a problem for me. I don't trust myself to write it, or I don't think I understand enough. Worse, I talk it away. "It's not that big a deal. Write what will make people happy."

That's writing scared, which is a conflict in and of itself, and it's also choosing to only tell a slice of the story.

We left Juliet deciding to take the potion that will put her in a state as though she is dead. Shakespeare could've chosen to write the ending so that all goes according to the Friar's plan: Juliet wakes up, the Capulets are thrilled she's alive and decide Romeo would be a fantastic son-in-law after all. Everyone lives happily ever after. (Except maybe Paris. Perhaps he could marry Rosaline.)

This is a tragedy, though—the mother of all conflicts. If Shakespeare ended this play happily, what would we make of Mercutio and Tybalt's deaths? What about the feud between the Capulets and Montagues, or the difficulties of being a teenager and those who parent them? Shrugging our shoulders and saying, "Let bygones be bygones," is refusing to see the entire story.

I might be scared and sad to move on to Acts 4 and 5. I might not understand or trust myself to help my students through a sorrowful set of events, but this is the story I have, so I will show my students how to walk in it.

I become a placeholder, and I do what Jesse did for Hadley over a decade ago. I hold up tiny pieces for my students to take steps towards, and together we pick them up and we talk about what it is we see when we look closely.

We start with the Nurse. She finds Juliet, a child she loves and has taken care of as her own, dead. By this point, we've studied inflection, pauses, and when an actor might use non-verbals when saying lines. The class is comfortable playing around with the lines to add drama and empathy to this scene. For example, we discuss how the Nurse might say, "Lady, lady, lady!" after she's drawn back the curtain, revealing Juliet. Some students read that line with a pause between "lady," and each time it becomes louder and more frantic as the Nurse realizes what's happened. Others speak this line quickly and with annoyance, as though Juliet's being a typical teenager and refusing to wake up in the morning. We do the same thing when Lady Capulet, Juliet's father, and Paris walk in and see Juliet lifeless. We talk about how we would act out Juliet's mother's lines: "O me, my child, my only life! Revive, look up, or I will die with thee!" Reading the play this way, making decisions about how we would say these lines, we put ourselves in the characters' place, and imagine how it would feel to see and react to Juliet's death.

When the Friar steps in, he has an opportunity to fix all this. He could tell the truth, explain what he's cooked up, but instead he speaks to the group as though he's conducting a funeral service, and explains what to do with the body.

I want to scream at the Friar, and I tell my students this.

I suppose my reaction confuses my class, since up until this point, my biases have lain with the kids in the play. This is not the case in this scene. I ache for the parents now, and I want to body-slam Friar Lawrence.

"Tell the truth!" I want to yell. "They may be imperfect parents, but aren't we all? They're still her parents. Tell the truth, and let them fix this, as a family, when Juliet wakes up." My reaction might confuse my students, but I'm showing them how to look at tragedy. Nothing in this story is easy. Everyone is right. Everyone is wrong. We learn to walk through the story holding onto both of these truths.

What happens next is strange. Juliet's parents, Paris, and the Friar exit the stage, leaving the Nurse and a group of musicians who were supposed to play at Juliet and Paris' wedding. The Nurse tells them to put away their instruments because right now, life is too sorrowful for music. "Honest good fellows, ah put up, put up," she tells them. "For well you know this is a pitiful case."

One of the musicians thinks the Nurse is referring to the case of his instrument, and not of Juliet's death. "Ay, by my troth," he says, "the case may be amended." I imagine the musician examining his violin case, shrugging his shoulders and saying, "Chill out lady, it can be fixed."

Then, the musicians begin to argue with Peter, who tells them to play something. It's a ridiculous, confusing, and humorous conversation. I laugh every time I read this last scene. I love the pun Shakespeare uses to create the "case" joke, and as the musicians begin to fight, I see them all as the middle-schoolers I love so: rowdy, belligerent, and talented, but only seeing what's right in front of them. The scene is strange because it's humorous. Why would Shakespeare make this part funny after all the sadness that just occurred?

I remember on 9/11, I was teaching 7th-grade English. After the news spread that morning, the staff decided to take a few minutes of each class to allow students to discuss what was going on—a weird situation to be in, since I myself had little understanding of the situation. When I found out the planes hit the towers in New York City, I walked out of my classroom, ran down the stairs, walked into the principal's office, picked up his phone, called my dad who was working in Chicago at the time, and begged him to come home. The very last thing I was thinking about was acting like an adult. I did not feel capable of managing myself and my feelings as well as those of my 7th graders. I think the Nurse in Romeo and Juliet would understand. Nevertheless, my classes and I talked, and I did my best to be a calm presence, though I was dizzy from the effort.

During one class, a student said he was afraid they would come to Goshen, Indiana, where we were, next. To that, his buddy patted him on the back, chuckled, and shook his head. "No worries, dude," he said, "our tallest building is a McDonald's."

The whole class, including the kid who voiced his fear, laughed. It felt so good to laugh.

I know Shakespeare was working within the confines of a two-hour time frame, and he needed to allow his actors time to change or catch their breath before they performed the final scene. The end of Act 4 was probably written for that reason. This is also the Nurse's last scene, so she can stay and talk to the musicians while the rest of the main characters leave.

It's a scene put in for timing, but Shakespeare makes this scene funny. We are at the edge of a mountain, standing on a boulder that has begun to roll off a cliff and there isn't a thing we can do to stop it. Why bother to make anything funny?

Perhaps this is a reprieve before the final act. Shakespeare makes us laugh before the real trouble begins (after all, Juliet's not really dead). Perhaps the juxtaposition of sadness and humor helps us see the tragedy more clearly. In this scene, the musicians have no clue what's just happened, and their ignorance feels like innocence. They have the luxury to mess around. Their pitiful cases have no effect on the music they can play.

I think both these explanations are reasonable, but I think there is a third option to consider. While tragedy might be linear, this doesn't mean we don't see anything but tragedy. Like my character Molly who unsuccessfully tried to take her mind off the pain of the fireball in her mouth by slapping her bathing suit straps against her shoulders, I think Shakespeare is showing us it's possible to feel more than one thing.

When it's time for Act 5, I show Julian Fellowes and Carlo Carlei's version of *Romeo and Juliet*. I like to show this version because it's a beautiful movie, but also because of the writer's and director's interpretation of the death of Romeo. The scene is particularly piercing because Juliet wakes up just as Romeo is dying, and, for a few seconds, they see each other. In the classes I've shown this film in, there has always been a collective gasp as we watch one die and one awake.

I show this scene because I think it helps to bring the story alive, but I also want my students to see what it looks like to *create* within a story they've been given. My students know

Romeo and Juliet was not a story Shakespeare made up. They know he changed the length of time the two were married, from three months to one day, for example, or that he teased out the personalities of the Nurse and Mercutio. The same is true for Fellowes and Carlei. In the edition of the play we use, there are no stage directions that suggest Juliet wakes up as Romeo dies. That is something Fellowes and Carlei chose to do, and I think this decision comes from an understanding of the plot, the characters' personalities, and how a tragedy works. Like Shakespeare, Fellowes and Carlei cannot change the ending of the play. This could be thought of like an algebraic equation—the answer, the outcome, must remain the same, but this doesn't mean there is one way to get to that outcome or discover a new way a number might work.

I want my students to understand this concept of creating within a story, because this is how I believe they begin to see the story for themselves.

This is why we make promptbooks, or silly sentences in iambic pentameter with candy hearts. This is why I assign lazy sonnets, have them create Juliet's tomb, and write their own sonnet about a monster who helps and haunts at the same time. It's all so they can see the story for themselves. Like Jesse did for Hadley, I am doing what I need to do so my students can walk independently. Despite my discomfort with conflict, I want to teach my students that the solution is not to avoid it, but rather to try to look at it long enough so we can create from it.

After a few weeks of stewing about my conflict-less story, I decided to take it out again and see what I could do with it.

I remembered Jesse's observation that I'd set up a beautiful world for the girls in the story, and his question: What will they do in it? I read the story carefully, walking along with the main character, and found places where she was feeling sad, or worried, or unsure, and instead of going into more detail, I'd glossed over them, or written the story so that something else would happen so that I wouldn't have to make the main character say what it was that bothered her.

The girl was beginning to believe she was stupid. She was turning eleven in a few months, and she'd known these friends since they were all five years old, when they all met in kindergarten. That was the first year they'd been divided into reading and math groups, and every year since, the main character stayed in the slower classes, while her friends moved up. The girl felt jealous of her friends. She was angry that she wasn't given fun books to read and projects or plays to put on after reading them. She was sad that reading was so hard for her and she didn't understand why. She thought she liked stories, but, lately, she'd begun to hate them.

I kept the fireball scene, but at one point in the story, the friends got into a fight. It had to do with who was stupid, and who wasn't; who was bossy, and who wasn't. There was name-calling, and hurt feelings, and the main character ended up walking home alone.

My other revision had to do with a map. I gave my main character a map of the greater Chicagoland area with Lake Michigan, the city, and the West Suburbs marked on it. She kept it folded neatly in her desk, and before bed, marked places she'd been, sometimes adding little notes on Post-its® describing that event: vanilla ice-cream cones dunked in cherry topping from the Custard Shop, Ridgeland park for sledding, the Oak Park conservatory to see the goldfish swimming in all that murky green.

She never took the map with her, because she wanted to learn North, South, East, and West without looking at the page. She didn't understand it that way, anyway. She needed a story—a placeholder—to mark that locale.

After the fight, as the girl walked home by herself, sad and lonely, she thought about how she would mark up her map when she got home. She thought about North, South, East, and West, and realized she knew which was which: East was the Sears Tower, where one afternoon her family piled into the car and raced toward it because they heard on the radio that a man dressed as Spiderman was climbing the [then] world's tallest skyscraper. West was the Ferrara Pan Candy factory where, for a quarter, the ladies would hand out brown paper lunch bags filled with piping hot jelly beans, their color leaking through the paper. The main character always ate the red ones first. To the North was school, where she rubbed her paper with her eraser until it tore, trying to get rid of her long division mistakes, and it was also where her music teacher, a Southern gentleman with the greatest twangy accent she'd ever heard, let her choreograph dance moves to the 5th grade performance of "It Was Sad When the Great Ship Went Down." And South was Rehm Pool, where she left her friends— all of them angry, but she hoped they were still her friends.

When she got home, she took the map from her desk and marked where she'd been and what had happened at each spot. She was sad and worried, but she was also realizing she was learning how to walk around and see the world by herself.

It was a story that was by no means a tragedy, but it brought with it a "glooming peace," as the Prince says about the morning Romeo and Juliet are found dead. While the two teenagers' deaths prompt their fathers to shake hands and end the feud, the Prince says we are to "go hence to have more talk of these sad things."

Talking about them helps us remember, and remembering helps us to understand, and understanding means we allow ourselves to be marked by the story—like a thumbtack on a map. Here's where we've been. Here's where we can go.

Activities

Chapter 1

For the free printable "Candy Hearts Couplets," visit
Tweetspeak Poetry at https://www.tweetspeakpoetry.com/
2017/03/10/romeo-juliet-kissing-fair-dragon-cave/

Chapter 3

The good people of Verona have once again been subjected
to a heated brawl between the Montagues and the Capulets,
and are counting on the talented writers at *Feyen Times Press*
to help them sort through the events of the day.

The Handouts

Below is your assignment. You will be put into groups once
you've completed your writing, and together, you will design
a newspaper.

(Note: I printed each assignment and put it in envelopes
with the students' last names on them, along with a lollipop
and a pencil. Following are all the assignments I came up
with and put in separate envelopes.)

• Exclusive Interview with Prince Escalus

You have a chance to sit down with the Prince after he's
given out his ultimatum to the brawling Capulets and
Montagues. What is his temperament, and what does he

think about this feud? Is there anything that can be done to mend it? Come up with a list of questions to ask the Prince, then get into his character, and write responses from his perspective.

• Exclusive Interviews with Lady Capulet and Lady Montague

You have the special task of sitting down with both Ladies Capulet and Montague, and trying to have a conversation. How did this fight begin and who is to blame? As you think of your questions, and how you will organize your writing, keep in mind these two women cannot stand each other, and will likely interrupt (or, at the least, use a few eye rolls) while the other is speaking. Have fun with this interview!

• News Correspondents

You are in charge of writing the who, what, where, when, why, and how of the fight in Verona. Stick to the facts, and feel free to use dialog and description from what you read in Act 1, Scene 1.

• Op-eds

You are a longtime resident of Verona, and you have a thought or two regarding the feud between the Capulets and the Montagues. Write an opinion piece explaining what you think and why you think this way.

Chapter 6

Queen Mab DIY Instructions

Mercutio spins a delightful and haunting tale about a made-up fairy who pays us visits when we dream. Now, it is your turn. Create a character who comes along to haunt or to help (or both!). Examples: a fairy that helps with home-work, a leprechaun that grants you speed on the soccer field, an ogre that always makes the best donuts.

You are to write a sonnet about your made-up creation. The guidelines are as follows:

- Your sonnet should be in iambic pentameter

- Your sonnet must follow the Shakespearean ABAB, CDCD, EFEF, GG pattern

- For final drafts, you will need to draw your character, so think about how your creation will look

To get you thinking:

- What does your character look like?

- Does your character arrive with anything?

- Is your character always around, or does she/he/it arrive at certain times?

- How does your character help?

- How does your character haunt?

- Does your character have any magical powers?

Now that you have a few ideas, begin to write your sonnet. Remember, get the ideas down first, then worry about rhyming and rhythm.

Chapter 9

Museum Exhibit Directions

You are in charge of the Romeo and Juliet Exhibit at the local museum, and you are being commissioned to put together a display on Act 2, Scenes 4-6 so students can walk through and understand the story. Each of you will be given a set of lines and you must complete the following task:

- Fill the large piece of paper entirely with sketches/drawings/color of the scene.

- Write a summary of the scene. Your summary should be at least five sentences long.

- Identify at least two examples of language tricks in the lines you were given. Write the line where you found the trick, and identify what that trick is.

- Identify what you believe are the most important three lines, and explain why those lines are important.

All of these tasks should be on your large piece of paper.

Chapter 13

Songs and Stories Paper

Choose one character in *Romeo and Juliet*, and match a song with him or her. Write a five-paragraph paper answering the following questions:

- What about the character matches the song? Use evidence from *Romeo and Juliet* as well as the lyrics.

- When would this character listen to this song? Or in what sort of situation that relates to your character would this song be played?

- What is the central message (theme) in this song, and how does that relate to the character?

- What is important about this song?

- What is important about this character?

Acknowledgements

Thank you to Laura Barkat, for giving me this project at a time when I couldn't remember what I loved about teaching. You helped me remember.

Thank you to Sara Barkat, for reading the manuscript, several times, and pointing out places that needed more, and places that needed less. Thank you for your patience and your keen eye.

Thank you to Michelle Wilgenburg, for providing great resources to help me teach *Romeo and Juliet*, and for always being willing to discuss the mechanics, the plot, and the themes in the play. You are a great mentor, and it was an honor to teach with you.

Thank you to Washington Christian Academy, for giving me an opportunity to teach middle school. There is no other place I have felt more at home in my work.

This story couldn't have happened without the students I got to teach, and so, to the 8th graders of 2014-2015, and 2015-2016: it was an honor to tread through this awkward, mysterious, horrifying, wonderful play with you. Thank you for your humor and your hard work. Thank you for your creativity and your vulnerability.

Thank you to my daughters, Hadley Grace and Harper Anne, for showing me the world again. You are my most powerful writing tools.

Thank you to Jesse, who years ago bought me a pack of pens, a notebook, and a subscription to a writing magazine for our wedding anniversary, and said, "You are always a mama; you're not only a mama." I'm sorry about all the other boys in this book. Since that August afternoon in 1995, there were none but you.

Notes

Epigraph

page 1   "...we will soon return to our tomorrow":
            Mahmoud Darwish, translated by Fady Joudah, from
            "We Were Missing a Present" in *The Butterfly's Burden*
            (Port Townsend, WA: Copper Canyon Press, 2007), p. 7.

Chapter 1

page 11   "Kissing a Dragon in His Fair Cave" first appeared at
            Tweetspeak Poetry, March 10, 2017, <https://www.tweet
            speakpoetry.com/2017/03/10/romeo-juliet-kissing-
            fair-dragon-cave/>

Chapter 14

page 94   "Act 4 belongs to Juliet": Peggy O'Brien, *Shakespeare Set
            Free* (New York: Washington Square Press, 1993), p. 179.

Bibliography

Gill, Roma, ed. *Romeo and Juliet*. Oxford: Oxford University Press, 2008.

O'Brien, Peggy, ed. *Shakespeare Set Free: Teaching Romeo & Juliet, Macbeth & A Midsummer Night's Dream*. New York: Washington Square Press, September 1, 1993.

Carlei, Carlo, dir. 2013. *Romeo and Juliet*. Icon Productions.

This book includes various references from or to the following companies, brands, and sources: *Delirious* written by Eddie Murphy, and directed by Bruce Gowers, 1983; the cologne Drakkar Noir by Guy Laroche, created by Pierre Wargnye, 1982; the hairspray Aqua Net; *Stand By Me*, directed by Rob Reiner, Columbia Pictures, 1986; the singer Howard Jones; the imitation whipped cream Cool Whip, introduced by Birds Eye division of General Foods in 1966; Chex Mix snack mix, produced by General Mills; "Dancing With Frankenstein" is from *The Faber Adventures Performance Piano Book*, by Nancy Faber and Randall Faber, Faber Piano Adventures, 1966; *Footloose*, directed by Herbert Ross, IndieProd Company Productions, 1984; "Uprising" is from the album *The Resistance* by Matthew Bellamy, Muse, 2009; "St. Matthew Passion, Passion Chorale" is from the album *Favorites from the Classics* Vol. 2, Bach, by Charles Gerhardt and the Ambrosian Singers; *Reader's Digest*, 2013; *Frankenstein* is by Mary Shelley, Lackington, Hughes, Harding, Marvos and Jones, 1818; Diet Coke, produced by The Coca-Cola Company, 1982; Tupperware, by Earl Tupper, 1948; Nutella, produced by Ferrero, 1964; Pac-Man is by Namco, 1980; *Hamilton* is by Lin-Manuel Miranda, The Public Theatre, 2015; *Jaws*, directed by Steven Spielberg, Zanuck/Brown Productions, 1975; Mack Trucks, by Jack and Augustus Mack, 1900; "Sorry" is from the album *Purpose*, by Julia Michael, Justin Tranter, Sonny Moore, Micheal Tucker, and Justin Bieber, Skrillex and Blood, 2015; "Hook" is from the album *Four* by John Popper, 1994; Keds, by Wolverine World Wide, 1916; "We Didn't Start the Fire" is from the album *Storm Front* by Billy Joel, Columbia, 1989; Target, 1902; the band One Direction, 2010; *To Kill a Mockingbird* is by Harper Lee, J.B. Lipponcott and Co., 1960; Netflix, founded by Reed Hastings and Marc Randolph, 1997; Gina's Italian Ice, Berwyn, Illinois, 1977; Oak Park Bakery, Inc.; Gossage Grill; *Nighthawks* is by Edward Hopper, Art Institute of Chicago, 1942; *Boulevard of Broken*

Dreams is by Gottfried Helnwein, 1984; *Where the Wild Things Are* is by Maurice Sendak, Harper and Row, 1964; "Ghost" is from the album *Rites of Passage* by the Indigo Girls, Epic, 1992; "Closer to Fine" is from the album *Indigo Girls*, Epic, 1989; Walkman is by Sony, 1979; Band-Aid is from Johnson & Johnson, 1920; *Beverly Hills 90210* is by Darren Star, produced Aaron Spelling, 1990; Chicago Cubs; Cheerios is by General Mills, 1941; IKEA; Hole in the Wall Ice-Cream Shoppe in Oak Park, Illinois; Oak Park Conservatory; Ferrara Pan Candy Company is owned by the Catterton Partners; "It Was Sad When The Great Ship Went Down," is by William and Versey Smith, 1927; "Sometimes" is by Mary Oliver, from the book *Red Bird*, Beacon Press, 2008; Mod Podge is a registered trademark of Plaid Enterprises, Inc; Post-it is a registered trademark of 3M; *Eleanor & Park* is a book by Rainbow Rowell, published by St. Martin's Press in 2013. *The Romeo and Juliet Code* is a book by Phoebe Stone, published by Scholastic Inc. in 2012. *The Wednesday Wars* is a book by Gary D. Schmidt, published by Houghton Mifflin Harcourt in 2009. Spotify is a streaming media system founded by Daniel Ek, and Martin Lorentzon in 2006.

Also from T. S. Poetry Press

Rumors of Water: Thoughts on Creativity & Writing, by L.L. Barkat (Twice named a Best Book of 2011)

A few brave writers pull back the curtain to show us their creative process. Annie Dillard did this. So did Hemingway. Now L.L. Barkat has given us a thoroughly modern analysis of writing. Practical, yes, but also a gentle uncovering of the art of being a writer.

– Gordon Atkinson, Editor at Laity Lodge

How to Write a Poem: Based on the Billy Collins Poem "Introduction to Poetry," by Tania Runyan

How to Write a Poem uses images like the buzz, the switch, the wave—from the Billy Collins poem "Introduction to Poetry"—to guide writers into new ways of writing poems. Excellent teaching tool. Anthology and prompts included.

The Joy of Poetry: How to Keep, Save & Make Your Life With Poems, by Megan Willome

An unpretentious, funny, and poignant memoir. A defense of poetry, a response to literature that has touched her life, and a manual on how to write poetry. I loved this book. As soon as I finished, I began reading it again.

– David Lee Garrison, author of *Playing Bach in the D.C. Metro*

Romeo & Juliet:
The Teacher Diaries Companion

"A love story, an epic tragedy, a cautionary tale about parents respecting their children, even, incredibly, more than a minor note of humor—*Romeo and Juliet* has it all."   —Sara Barkat, editor

Encounter the play *Romeo & Juliet* in the company of four vibrant women who love stories and ideas: Sara Barkat, Callie Feyen, Hannah Haney, and Karen Swallow Prior.

At turns thoughtful, informative, personal, or funny, these are voices that will draw you into a timeless work and transform Shakespeare into more than just an old playwright you were (or are) compelled to read.

This volume includes the play, essays, personal annotations by Callie Feyen, four bonus classroom activities, and a glossary.

The Teacher Diaries Series

The Teacher Diaries Series gives you the inside scoop
on the heart, mind, and soul of teachers—as they go about
the hard and beautiful task of raising our children to be
smart, creative, thoughtful, and kind.

T. S. Poetry Press titles are available online in e-book and print
editions. Print editions also available through Ingram.

tspoetry.com